PLURALISTIC PORTRAIT of God

PLURALISTIC PORTRAIT of GOD
Copyright © 2023 by LISA W. BUGAYONG

Published in the United States of America
ISBN   Paperback: 978-1-959761-58-7
ISBN   eBook: 978-1-959761-59-4

All rights reserved. No part of this publication may be reproduced, stored in a retrieval system or transmitted in any way by any means, electronic, mechanical, photocopy, recording or otherwise without the prior permission of the author except as provided by USA copyright law.

The opinions expressed by the author are not necessarily those of ReadersMagnet, LLC.

ReadersMagnet, LLC
10620 Treena Street, Suite 230 | San Diego, California, 92131 USA
1.619. 354. 2643 | www.readersmagnet.com

Book design copyright © 2023 by ReadersMagnet, LLC. All rights reserved.

Cover design by Kent Gabutin
Interior design by Daniel Lopez

PLURALISTIC PORTRAIT of God

LISA W. BUGAYONG

ReadersMagnet, LLC

Dedicated to my family, Jeffrey, Alexandra, Elizabeth, Rosemary, whose support and love make all things possible for me.

TABLE OF CONTENTS

Sacred Text Reference 1

CHAPTER 1:   Searching for Meaning 2

CHAPTER 2:   Judaism-God is Involved in the World....................... 14

CHAPTER 3:   Islam-God is the Single Creator 35

CHAPTER 4:   Christianity-God is Love.. 55

CHAPTER 5:   Hindism-God is the Conciousness of All Reality....... 74

CHAPTER 6:   Buddhism-God is Peace... 97

CHAPTER 7:   Taoism-God is the Energy of Life...............................121

CHAPTER 8:   Conclusion 148

SACRED TEXT REFERENCES

—All quotes from the Bible refer to: *Holy Bible*. New Living Translation. Carol Stream, IL: Tyndale House Publishers, Inc., 2004

—All quotes from the Upanishads refer to: *The Upanishads, Breath of the Eternal*. Translated by Swami Prabhavananda, and Frederick Manchester. New York: The New American Library, Inc., 1957

—All quotes from the Tao Te Ching refer to: Chen, Ellen M. *The Tao Te Ching*. St. Paul: Paragon House, 1989

—All quotes from the Qur'an refer to: *The Glorius Qur'an*. Translated by the Translation Committee including: Prof. Dr. Ali Ozek, Prof. Dr. Nureddin Uzunoglu, Doc. Dr. Tevfik Rustu Topuzoglu, and Prof. Dr. Mehmet Maksutoglu. Istanbul, 2003

—All quotes from the Tanakh refer to: *Tanakh, The Holy Scriptures*, The New JPS Translation According to the Traditional Hebrew Text. Philadelphia: The Jewish Publications Society, 1985

—All quotes from the Bhagavad-Gita refer to: *The Bhagavad-Gita, Kirshna's Counsel in Time of War*. Translated by Barbara Stoler Miller. New York: Bantam Dell, 2004

—All quotes from the *Rig Veda* refer to the website: Internet Sacred Text Archive, Hinduism, *Rig Veda*, translated by Ralph Griffith. <www.sacred-texts.com/hin/index.htm>

—All quotes from the Tao Te Ching refer to: Chen, Ellen M. The Tao Te Ching, A New Translation with Commentary. St. Paul: Paragon House, 1989

CHAPTER 1:
SEARCHING FOR MEANING

The search for God has permeated every society all over the globe since the dawn of humanity. Humans, unlike animals, have the capability to ponder and wonder about life, and with that ability they have created religions that have sought answers to the recurring questions, "Why are we here?" "Who gave us life?" and "Who ordered the universe?" Or, in other words, "What or who is God?" In our technologically advanced age, some scientist and philosophers have renounced the very idea of God, claiming that humans invented God to quiet our own fears. It is true that the realities of life are certainly scary. Natural disasters, change, sickness, and ultimately death keep us constantly seeking a protector, a savior. We wonder if death is the end of life, hoping for eternal salvation with God.

Studying the earliest religions seems to point to this very understanding of God as a human Creation. These primitive religions used magic and superstition to try to ease the fears of everyday life.

Amulets and talismans were used to heal or ward off sicknesses. Fears about the future were calmed with the invention of astrology and divination. Some used sacrifice to appease angry gods or fix cosmic problems. Burial rituals were created to assure believers a good standing in the next life. Most ancient religions had myths that described gods who were similar to humans; for example, they had wives, children, territories, and responsibilities that looked much like ours. Common amongst these religions was also the idea that the greatest god was associated with the powerful king or emperor of the time. This appears to be just an extension of own our human ways.

At times, like many I suppose, I have questioned my own faith, yet something keeps tugging at my soul. What continues to give me confidence in God is the realization that the gates between the divine and humanity were blown open during the time period between 800-200 BC.[1] It appears that God actually made contact with humans. We need only to listen to the voices in all the sacred literature of that time to see that certain people truly believed that they had connected with something beyond humanity. It's as if God had finally had enough of our childish ways and cried, "Look, here I am, and I am greater than you ever imagined." Worldwide new ideas sprouted up enlarging our understanding of ourselves and God, and these divinely inspired beliefs became the foundation of the major religions that still thrive today.

In China, the writer of the *Tao Te Ching* was touched by something divine. This mystical encounter left him feeling disconnected from the ordinary hustle and bustle of the world. In the *Tao Te Ching*, he tried to explain his experience. "The multitudes are busy and active, like partaking of the sacrificial feast, like ascending the platform in spring; I alone am bland . . . the multitudes all have too much, I alone am deficient. . . . The multitudes all have their use; I alone am untamable like lowly material. I alone am different from others. For I treasure feeding on the mother." (20.3-5) His new awareness of life opened his eyes to the futility of most normal, everyday activities as compared to the ultimate experience he found in the Mother. India was home to Siddhartha Gautama, the Buddha, who had a mystical experience which he termed "enlightenment." It enabled him to understand the reality of the universe. He explained it as such: "I attained the undefiled supreme security from bondage, Nibbana. The knowledge and vision arose in me: 'My liberation is unshakable.'" (*Mijjhima-Nikaya* 26.18)[2] Also, the sages in India, who created the Upanishads, declared that their soul was a direct link to God. One proclaimed, "The truth is that you are always united with the Lord, but you must know this. Nothing further is there to know." (*Svetasvatara* 1.12) Another said, "Brahman is the soul in each; he indeed is the self in all. He is all." (*Brihadaranyaka* 5.1) The prophets of Israel also had a profound experience with God. Jeremiah experienced a feeling of being called by God from birth. "The

Lord gave me this message: I knew you before I formed you in your mother's womb. Before you were born I set you apart and appointed you as my prophet to the nations." (Jer 1:4-5) The prophet Ezekiel claimed that "the heavens were opened and I saw visions of God." (Ez 1:1) Religiously there was never such an explosive time period as this one deemed the axial period.

Later, at the beginning of the Common Era, there was another major religious breakthrough. A man named Jesus was given the title "Son of God" by his followers. He received that title because that is how he perceived himself. "Don't you believe that I am in the Father and Father is in me? The words I speak are not my own, but my Father who lives in me does his work through me. Just believe that I am in the Father and the Father is in me." (Jn 14:10-11) He saw a direct connection between himself and his Father, which was none other than the one God in heaven. After his crucifixion and resurrection, one of his faithful followers, Paul, made the bold statement, "I received my message from no human source, and no one taught me. Instead, I received it by direct revelation from Jesus Christ." (Gal 1:12)

About six hundred years later, another important prophet emerged. Muhammad explained to the Arabs, "O mankind! Surely I am the messenger of Allah (God) to you all; Him to whom belongs the sovereignty of the heavens and the earth." (Q 7:158) He asserted that his teachings came directly from the Angel Gabriel. These people who where founders of a new religion were either all crazy, or they were touched by something that we have given the name, "God." Simply stated then, it was God who instituted all the major religions that people still follow today.

The time has come for another spiritual growth spurt. The world is on the brink of launching into a new era. This will not result in a new religion, but a better understanding of the religions that we have today. Religious people everywhere are beginning to realize that their faith may not be the only path to God. The barriers between faiths are breaking apart, opening the way for respect and tolerance to flow freely. New ideas, however, do not effortlessly seep into society. With the creation of each of the major religions, there was division and anger between the people who wanted to cling to the old ways, and those who were willing to invest in the new. The same growing pains can be seen today as the opposing group to religious pluralism, the fundamentalists, are tightening the reigns and trying to grasp on harder to a dying concept. That is the idea that only one religion is correct and holds all the absolute truths about God. This exclusivist argument can be convincing since it is based on the inconsistencies between the religions. Because there are contradictions, they argue, only one faith can be correct; therefore, it is imperative that you chose the right one, (their faith of course) or suffer the consequences.

If it is true that all the major faiths really come from God, then why would they have contradictions? One would expect differences, yes, but ideologies that are incompatible with each other doesn't make sense. There are two different ways to reconcile this problem. The first is to accept that God can still be found even among contradictions. This may seem like an odd statement, but even within religious traditions themselves, there are contradictions that are accepted as normal. For example, the very foundation of Christianity is built on the idea that God is three and also one. Huh? How do Christians make sense of this? They don't; they accept it as a mystery of God. Christianity is not the only religion with a contradiction in it. The *Tao Te Ching* explains to the Taoist, "Act by no-action. Then, nothing is not in order." (3.3) To those who are not Taoist, this statement is probably meaningless. How would one go about acting, but not acting? The Taoists, however, understand the deeper meaning denoted within this paradox. In Hinduism, the *Katha Upanishad* tells them, "What is within is also without. What is without is also within." (2.1.10) In this quote, the "within" is the individual's soul and the "without" represents the rest of the outside world. The *Chandogya Upanishad* clarifies this, "As large as the universe outside, even so large is the universe within the lotus of the heart. Within it are heaven and earth, the sun, the moon, the lightning, and all the stars. What is in the macrocosm is in this microcosm." (8.1.3) Here again, an important spiritual concept is revealed through a contradiction. Hindus realize that logically this is unreasonable, but spiritually it makes perfect sense. It appears that even within individual religions God uses contradictions to unveil parts of himself.

The second way of fixing this problem is probably viewed by some as heretical. Yet, I propose that it is important to realize that over the years mistakes about God have crept into our religions. Therefore, correcting past errors could have the capability of fixing some of the contradictions. These mistakes have been handed down from one generation to the next through the sacred scriptures. This is one area that needs to be reevaluated. The scriptures have created a dam that blocks exclusivists from expanding their limited view of life. The exclusivists cling to their own book and assess the world through the eyes of its contents. This is, in my opinion, the main cause of religious intolerance, religious wars, and all the terror that religion has done to innocent people in the name of upholding the sacred word of God. All the sacred works were written hundreds, if not thousands of years ago when we were still spiritual infants. Does one look back at what they wrote as a child and think that it is perfect, and everything that they have learned since should be tossed out as meaningless and forgotten? In order to progress toward becoming more spiritually mature, toward working for a better community, a better world, it is imperative that we recognize that our sacred books, all of them, are sacred because they were inspired by God. This does not mean, however, that these books are free from errors. God himself inspired the writers of all the sacred literature, but some of the message got distorted between God and the writer's pen. God had only fallible humans to reveal his message to; they could not help but be influenced by the culture of their time. So we read in these documents that slavery is a natural part of life, that woman are secondary to men, and that violence in the name of religion is deemed necessary by God. Not one sacred scripture is free from the human perception of the world. Yet, even within in the muddy contents of human error, God still shines through these pages. The problem is sorting out the human ideas from God's. This is the challenge to our generation. This is a required necessity for pluralism to thrive today. We as humans must have the humility to accept that we have made errors in the past, and realize that we must fix those errors today. Otherwise, religion will stagnate and pluralism will die.

Being open to the new age idea of pluralism is an important step in answering the ultimate question, "Who is God?" The divine is such an awesome concept that to try to fit all parts of it equally into one religion would clutter it and make it difficult for people to understand. Therefore, it appears that each religion has chosen to focus in on only one important aspect of God, with all the others still there, but overshadowed by the key characteristic. The only way, then, to get a full picture of God, is to put all the pieces together as if they are all part of one large puzzle. In this way, we can realize that each of the major religions today including Christianity, Islam, Hinduism, Buddhism, Taoism, and Judaism are all necessary parts of the whole picture. With the help of devoted followers, each faith can take their understanding of God and nurture it into a beautiful flower, and maybe, with some time and patience, the entire world will be one big garden planted by God. It will be a garden where no one flower overtakes another, but each living in harmony with the other and creating an overall beautiful picture of who God is.

In the following chapters, I look to each of the major faiths individually to explore their personal definition of the divine. It must be mentioned though, here at the outset, that I am not trying to explain all the wisdom contained within a specific religion. There are many books already available that do that. I am trying to illuminate the one characteristic about God within each faith that seems to be the driving factor upon which most (but probably not all) theology, rituals, and practices are based. In each chapter, the process of how the religion evolved and based itself on that idea about God is explored, and how it is continuously relevant to the religion.

BIBLIOGRAPHY

1. Hick, John. *God Has Many Names*. Philadelphia: Westminster Press, 1982. p. 45
2. Bodhi, Bhikkhu, ed. *In the Buddha's Words, An Anthology of Discourses from the Pali Canon*. Boston: Wisdom Publications, 2005. p. 59

CHAPTER 2:
JUDAISM—GOD IS INVOLVED IN THE WORLD

God's invisibility is a defining part of his personality. He is the ultimate mystery. This, of course, can be a barrier to understanding who God really is. With people, we can immediately see if someone is fun and boisterous or the more shy, demure type. With God, however, we must peer more carefully beneath the surface to know his personality. The clues to understanding God are around us, claim the Jews. For God does not just sit in heaven with popcorn in hand and watch humans like a television show; that would mean we were created for mere entertainment. Not so, cry the Jews! God loves the people he made, and so he is intimately involved in life. God's feelings for humanity and his glorious will can be deduced by looking to his actions. Within this framework then, Jews look to the events of the world to seek knowledge about God. The divine is not some natural law, or just some awesome mysterious power of the universe, but has personal characteristics. God is someone who can love, protect, and redeem the Jewish Nation. These are the characteristics of God that the Jews experienced personally, and so they stand at the center of their faith.

The Jews believe they can physically see God's devotion through his actions. God is involved with his Creation; because of this it is God that drives history and, therefore, the fate of the world. Sometimes God may work through individuals by guiding them to his will, and other times God may require something stronger like a miracle. The Hebrew Tanakh is full of these supernatural events. These are the target points in history where God's intervention for the Jews is obvious, and they are proof of God's love for them. Not only does God help the Jews as a nation, but the Tanakh also shows how he comes to the aid of individuals as well. God cares so much that he is constantly working toward helping humans to redeem themselves from their own wickedness.

If this was not the case, many people would give up on life, because it would simply be a meaningless, chaotic show of events. But because we can depend on God to redeem us, a divorce can mean a new beginning and a chance for a better relationship with someone else. The death of a loved one might draw a family closer. A natural disaster could bring a country together to rebuild a city. Events have meaning, and sometimes they even give us a glimpse of our Creator.

Of course, the Hebrew Tanakh is full of the liveliest miracles, but even now in our modern times I believe there are still miracles happening. In our present culture, though, we look to other sources of explanations besides God, and therefore have slammed the door shut of any spiritual influence in our lives. We need only to open the door to see that God is still active and constantly working for the world's redemption. This is the characteristic of God which the Jews see as most important. This truth is like a single, yet double-sided coin. The first side reminds people that God has been active in human affairs in the past, and will continue to do so in the present and future. The flip side of the coin is that as God is active, so must humans be. This idea is incorporated in the Jewish covenant. This covenant is a pact between God and man working together for the redemption of the world.

The idea of redemption begs the question, "Redeemed from what?" Did God make a mistake when he made humans? It would appear that way. Right from the start the first human, Adam, disobeyed God and was thrown out of his perfect dwelling place, the Garden of Eden. Then the very next story in the bible tells us that Adam's son, Cain, attacked and killed his brother, Able. From there, the world spiraled out of control. According to the Hebrew Tanakh, "The Lord saw how great was man's wickedness on earth, and how every plan devised by his mind was nothing but evil all the time. And the Lord regretted that He had made man on earth, and His heart was saddened." (Gen

6:5-6) But, if as the first chapter of Genesis tells the Jews, "God saw all that he had made, and found it very good," (Gen 1:31) then how could the human species have become so rotten to the core? To comprehend this better, it is necessary to understand the Jewish philosophy about the creation of humans. The Jews believe that humans were created by God with two conflicting tendencies. In the Talmud it explains to them, "The Holy One, Blessed be He, created two impulses, one good and the other evil." (Ber. 61a)$_1$ Why would a good, loving God produce people with an evil nature? The Jews believe that people were not created to be God's puppets completely controlled by his strings, so God gave humans free will. In order for people to consciously decide to be good, there must also be the bad to choose from as well. Good does not exist in a vacuum. Good is only defined as "good" because it is the opposite of bad. For this reason, God allows evil in the world.

Early in history, humans failed in their struggle to choose the more difficult path of righteousness. Therefore, selfishness, greed, and hatred ruled the world. In this environment, people were too busy to hear an invisible God; however, there was one man who still had an ear for God—Noah. According to the Jews, a person who can actually hear God speaking to them is called a prophet. This is an important concept to Judaism. It shows that God is constantly trying to communicate and stay involved in the world. Prophets who hear his message are then expected to take it to the people. Noah's message, however, was not heard and so God washed away the filth from the earth with a great flood. God did not, however, give up on humans. He saved the human race through Noah and his ark.

After the flood, God first introduced the idea of the covenant. It began as a simple agreement between Noah and God that he would never flood the world again. "I have set My bow in the clouds, and it shall serve as a sign of the covenant between Me and the earth. When I bring clouds over the earth, and the bow appears in the clouds, I will remember My covenant between me and you and every living creature among all flesh, so that the waters shall never again become a flood to destroy all flesh." (Gen 9:13-15) But God had bigger plans for humanity then just pure survival.

The covenant between God and the Jewish people is the underlying theme that is developed in the first four books of the Hebrew Tanakh. The true beginnings of Judaism have their roots in the covenant made between God and Abraham. God found in Abraham a man worthy of helping him enlarge the idea of the covenant. It was Abraham who, without question, moved from his homeland to Canaan because the Lord asked him to. Now, the covenant was based on recognizing that God has humanity's best interest at heart in everything he does and asks people to do. The Tanakh says that Abraham had "put his trust in the Lord, (and) He reckoned it to his merit." (Gen 15:6) The covenant did not disappear; it was passed on to Isaac, Abraham's son.

Isaac had two children of his own, and through his younger son, Jacob, the covenant survived.

Jacob had twelve sons of his own who each became the head of an Israelite tribe, and together they are called the twelve tribes of Israel. The tribes settled in Egypt, and there they grew in numbers until the king began to worry about their increase. He realized that in time of war the Israelites might not support him, and he would be outnumbered. Upon this recognition, the king decided to force the Israelites into becoming slaves for him. After many years of slavery, the "Israelites were groaning under the bondage and cried out; and their cry for help from the bondage rose up to God. God heard their moaning, and God remembered His covenant with Abraham and Isaac and Jacob." (Ex 2:23-24)

God chose to intervene in human affairs on the behalf of the Israelites. Through a burning bush God revealed himself to Moses, and gave him the task of delivering his people from slavery. Moses led the people through the desert and into the promise land of Canaan. It was at Mt. Sinai, a camp site in the desert, where the crowning development of the covenant happened. God had decided that the Israelites were now in a more mature place with him, and it was time to give them the Law. It occurred miraculously with "thunder and lighting, and a dense cloud upon the mountain, and a very loud blast of the horn . . ." (Ex 19:16) and God "said to Moses, 'Come up to Me, on the mountain and wait there, and I will give you the stone tablets with the teachings and commandments which I have inscribed to instruct them.'" (Ex 24:12) The Jews look back at this event and consider it similar to a wedding day between God and his people. God's laws are compared to a wedding gift from the bridegroom to his new bride.$_2$ The Law had the effect of forever changing the covenant from a one-way dirt road into a two-way highway. The covenant was now an appropriate vehicle for the partnership between God and man working together in propelling the world toward righteousness. It was also a constant reminder of appropriate behavior that would keep the Israelites from falling prey to their weaker side. The Talmud reminds the Jews, "My children, I have created the evil impulse, and I have created the Torah as an antidote to it; if you occupy yourselves with Torah you will not be delivered into its power." (Kid 30b)$_3$ The Torah, the first four books of the Hebrew Tanakh, is equivalent to the Law in Judaism. With this Law, each individual now had the capability to see clearly how God expected them to behave.

The Israelites built a dwelling ark and placed the covenantal laws inside. They carried it with them as they journeyed to their new land of Canaan. Later, after they had established the Nation of Israel, they built a temple and put the covenantal laws inside the center of the temple in the holies of holies. The temple itself and the sacrificial part of the Law done therein began to overshadow the moral code. The Jews understood their holiness before God to be tied to their sacrifices, and their morals began to decline. Over time, they began to accept and believe in the gods of the surrounding tribes.

In response to these problems, God once again took the reins and sent his message to the prophets. They raged against the moral decline of society. Hosea declared that God proclaimed, "I desire goodness, not sacrifice; obedience to God, rather than burnt offerings." (Hosea 6:6) Isaiah also spoke for God saying, "'What need have I of all your sacrifices?' says the Lord. 'I am sated with burnt offerings of rams, and suet of Fatlings, and blood of bulls; and I have no delight in lambs and he-goats.'" (Is 1:11) "Learn to do good. Devote yourselves to justice; aid the wrong. Uphold the rights of the orphan; defend the cause of the widow." (Is 1:17) The Jews had broken their covenant with God; they were no longer working with God to redeem the world. They had fallen into the same pattern from earlier times that had led to the destructive flood. God tried to fix things by sending the prophets, but people refused to listen. God could not send a flood to destroy the earth, but neither could he let the people continue in their immoral ways. The prophets proclaimed to the people that if they did not change their evil ways then God would ultimately judge them and cause their doom. In 586 BC, it was no surprise to the prophets when Babylon conquered Judah. The Babylonians destroyed the temple, and deported most of Jews from their homeland. The prophets had made it clear that this was their punishment. Jeremiah told the people that God said, "This shall be your lot, your measured portion from Me. Because you forgot Me and trusted in falsehood." (Jer 13:25)

Just as God had intervened to save them through Moses, he also judged them and found them guilty causing their downfall. The Jews see God's hand in all events; things happen because God wills it. Therefore, history is a roadmap to God. But God is not only found in the past, but in the present and future. The Israelites accepted defeat because it came from God, but the prophets gave them hope and assured them that it would not remain that way forever. They delivered the message to the people that God had allowed them to be overtaken and deported, but at the same time God still loved them and would eventually restore Israel to her former beauty. Isaiah told the people, "Can a woman forget her baby, or disown the child of her womb? Though she might forget, I never could forget you." (Is 49:15)

The prophets didn't stop at restoration; their vision went beyond that to complete redemption of Israel. In fact, Israel's liberation would also bring about the world's redemption. The vision of the prophet's future, perfect world became solidified in the idea of a messianic age. Isaiah tells the Jews about this future event. "They shall beat their swords into plowshares and their spears into pruning hooks. Nations shall not take up sword against nation; They shall never again know war." (Is 2:4) This new hope, along with their Torah, was like the glue that would hold the Jews together through all the trials they still had to endure.

The Jews were finally allowed, under Persian rule around 500 BC, to return to Israel, yet they were still a crushed nation. They were hanging onto their faith by a tether that was frayed to just a thread. It was Ezra who provided the leadership they needed; he seemed to have a natural capacity for understanding what it would take to keep the Jewish faith alive. He put his trust in the Torah, and with it renewed the Jewish commitment to the covenant. The Rabbis declared, "Ezra was worthy that the Torah should be given to Israel by his hand," (Sanh 21b) and "When the Torah had been forgotten by Israel, Ezra came up from Babylon and reestablished it."(Suk 20a) He recognized that saving the Jewish faith depended on the people dedicating their entire lives to the Torah. The Jewish manner of worship, their home, their daily acts, and every detail of Jewish life would henceforth be based completely on the Torah.[4] In this fashion, following the Law became one of the most important tenants of the Jewish faith.

The exile and return, along with Ezra's leadership, were the catalyst that started a change in the Jewish faith. The new focus of the religion became the Torah or Jewish Law. During the time of exile, the synagogue, a place to pray and study the Torah, replaced the temple which was unavailable in Babylon. Since they could no longer sacrifice animals to gain purity in the presence of the Lord this ritual became obsolete. Keeping the Law replaced sacrifices as the way to sanctification. Rabbis, people learned in the Torah, replaced priests who had overseen the sacrifices. Those who followed these new institutions became known as Pharisees. The other form of Judaic worship was the old-fashioned temple sacrifices and priests. This type of Judaism resumed once the Jews came back to Israel and rebuilt their temple. These Jews were called Sadducees. For many years, these two sects of Judaism lived side by side.

The Jews, with only a brief interlude of independent rule, went from the hands of the Persians, to the Greeks, and then to the Romans. The Jews longed for their independence and suffered terribly from Roman persecution. By 66 CE, they could bear their situation no longer and finally revolted against the Roman government. The Jews fought hard against the monstrous Roman army, but in the end they were almost completely annihilated and their second temple destroyed in 70 CE. The destruction of the temple hit the Sadducees the hardest as they were dependent on the temple for their sacrifices and unification of their followers. After the temple was gone, so were the Sadducees, only the Pharisees lived on to continue the Judaic religion.[5]

Judaism's transformation was complete and it had developed into a religion based mostly on the scriptures and the Law therein. As a minority in the world, the Jews clung to their scriptures as a unifying symbol of their Judaism. Studying these documents became an important way to grasp a hold of fragile faith. The scriptures were a place filled with memories of how God made a covenant with his people and continued to interact with them throughout history.

The Tanakh was the first and most influential scripture written. The first five books of the Tanakh are called the Torah and they include: Genesis, Exodus, Leviticus, Numbers, and Deuteronomy. These books together have the lead part; they contain the 613 laws from God. The rest of the Tanakh is like the chorus which is in harmony with the Torah and adds fullness to it. The prophet books are packed with words from the various prophets including Joshua, Judges, I Samuel, II Samuel, I Kings, II Kings, and the later prophets of Isaiah, Jeremiah, Ezekiel, plus twelve other minor ones. The writings books follow the prophets; this is where the emotional, creative expression of the Jews comes out in prayers, stories, poems, and philosophical treatises about God. The writing books include: Psalms, Proverbs, Job, Song of Songs, Ruth, Lamentations, Ecclesiastes, Esther, Daniel, Ezra, Nehemiah, I Chronicles, and II Chronicles.

Along side the Tanakh, the Jews also had ideas that were passed down orally. The oral law was traditionally believed to be given to Moses, and passed down through the prophets to the elders, and then to the Sages and Rabbis. It was an expansion and explanation of the written law in the Torah. In order to keep the Torah at the center of Judaism, these ideas were at first transmitted only orally. The oral law would have continued in this fashion except that history was not kind to the Jewish people. After the first Jewish war and the destruction of their temple, the Jews' situation did not improve; it degenerated even further. The Jews were adamant about winning their freedom from the Romans, and went on to lose two more wars against their enemy. After the final war, the Roman Emperor, Hanadrian, hated the Jews enough to ban them from Jeruselum.[6] Under these chaotic conditions, the Rabbis made the difficult decision, against their better judgment, to write down the oral law. It was about 200 BC when Rabbi Yhudah HaNasi finished what was called the *Mishnah*. This was not the end, but the beginning of the oral law. Rabbis continued to make oral additions to the *Mishnah* which became known as *Germara*. Later, the *Germara* and *Mishnah* were edited into one book called the Talmud. The Tanakh and the Talmud are the two sacred scriptures of the Jews.

According to the Tanakh, "God created man in His image, in the image of God He created them; male and female He created them." (Gen 1:27) This passage permeates throughout all of Jewish theology. The exact meaning of the passage is still being debated. Is it a human's reasoning capabilities, emotions, or our free choice that resembles God? Or is it a conglomeration of all of these things making up our individual personalities? The nuts and bolts of it may continue to be argued throughout the ages, but the ultimate meaning of the passage points to the holiness of humans. Every precious, adorable little infant is born with an imprint of the divine on their soul. From the moment of birth, humans are linked to God by a likeness shared between them. Being born holy is one thing, but to maintain that holiness requires a constant struggle. Every day a Jew must reaffirm their commitment to be holy and work with God. In this way, they say "YES" to God's covenant. For the Lord spoke to Moses and said, "You shall be holy, for I, the Lord your God, am holy." (Lev 19:2)

Keeping the Jewish Law and performing good deeds is the path to holiness. The Jewish Law is made up of 613 commandments outlined throughout the Torah. These laws regulate all parts of a Jewish life from their diet to their sexual life, as well as business interactions, home life, prayer, and rituals for celebrating Jewish feast days. This is the Jew's guide for how to keep their covenant with God. The Law is also important on a more global scale as well. The Jews believe that their piety in following God's Laws will eventually bring about the coming of the Messiah. This will be the new age when love and peace shall reign. In this way, the Jews understand themselves to be partners with God both working together toward a more righteous world.

The Law contains not just rules for ethical conduct, but also for ritual behavior as well. Rituals are a key aspect of the Jewish faith. The numerous laws and rituals in Judaism may cause those on the outside of this faith to see it as a dry religion void of any feeling or passion for God. This, however, is an unfair judgment of Judaism. For, in fact, the

Jewish community feels just the opposite about their rituals. The Jewish community is built on tradition which is what binds them together as a holy community in a covenant with God. They feel a connection to other Jews when they wear a tallit katan during morning prayer, or light candles on a Friday night. The rituals bring structure and security to a Jew's life. But they are also more than that; they are silent pointers to God. A simple lit candle can be a symbol of hope and redemption. It goes beyond words and symbolically shows the glory and wonder of God that sometimes words cannot convey.

The Jewish rituals are mostly associated with the Sabbath and other holidays. Celebrating festivals is a way to stop the roller coaster of everyday life and remember to enjoy God's blessings. Most of these festivals are meant also to remind Jews about the special moments between God and his people. These are the specific times when God reached out in a miraculous way and touched his people, setting them on the right path. Remembering these special moments is like sharing important memories with a friend or a spouse. Most married couples have fond memories of the day they met, or the day they became engaged. In a similar fashion, the Jewish festivals are like pulling out the family album and reliving the events of the past, and sharing the special moments that their ancestors experienced with God. The Jews, like no other religion, look to the past to understand God. Their early history is laid out in the Tanakh, which reminds them of God's constant intervention with the world to help his people. God's faithfulness in the past gives Jews assurance that he will continue to be faithful to them in the future.

The Sabbath whisks Jews back to the beginning of time when God performed his first act of love for humanity—Creation. It took God six days to fashion his masterpiece. "God blessed the seventh day and declared it holy, because on it God ceased from all the work of creation that He had done." (Gen 2:3) In this way, God role-modeled appropriate behavior. Jews too were expected to work for six days providing for themselves and their families but on the seventh day, they needed to stop and remind themselves of things beyond this world and ponder on the spiritual.

The Sabbath is much more than just a mere day of relaxation, in fact, honoring the Sabbath is what defines a Jew. According to the Talmud, "Breaking the Sabbath is like worshipping idols." (Yad Shabbos 30:15)[7] And the Torah reminds the Jews that "Whoever does work on it, that person shall be cut off from among his kin." (Ex 31:14) Why is the Sabbath so central to Judaism? Why is resting after the sixth day so important that to do otherwise would separate one from his people? The mystery of the Sabbath lies underneath the surface and finding out what made the seventh day so special. The Torah explains, "On the seventh day God finished the work that He had been doing." (Gen 2:2) This means that Creation was not actually completed until the seventh day. But what did God do on the seventh day that caused it to become favored and holy? He gifted the world with something that was very important; it was not a physical dimension, but a spiritual one. In a way God added himself to the world making it his own and giving it tranquility and harmony.[8] The seventh day then brought maximum completion to Creation and made it a worthy place for humans to dwell. When humans observe the Sabbath, they have an opportunity to enjoy the unity between God and Creation. For Jews, the "rest" of the Sabbath is really about being at peace with the world around them, and no longer trying to dominate or control it. This peace emulates the messianic age. In that future world, peace won't be just a once-a-week occurrence, but everyone at all times will be at peace with each other, Creation, and God.[9]

In addition to the Sabbath, The Torah also gives the Jews five other major holidays that they celebrate throughout the year. These include:

1. Rosh Hashanah—the Jewish new year.
2. Yom Kippur—the day of atonement
3. Succoth—fall harvest
4. Pesach—Passover
5. Shavuot—the gift of the law

Rosh Hashanah, like the Sabbath, has Creation as its central theme. The Jews bring in their new year celebrating the "birthday of the world," the day on which God breathed life into the first human, Adam. With God's role as Creator clearly defined, Jews are reminded of their dependency on God. A blast from the shofar (horn of a ram) announces to the Jews God's sovereignty. The shofar is sounded one hundred times during synagogue service on Rosh Hashanah. It's not only blown to announce God as their king, but also to awaken Jews to the implications of what that means within their own lives. This day is a mixture of the joys of creations and the somberness in remembering how mankind has fallen short of God's expectations for them. Over the next ten days, Jews are expected to spend time in self-reflection of their own personal shortcomings. This is a time to look back over the last year and recall their own failure to observe their covenant with God.

Following this is Yom Kippur, a very important Jewish holiday. It may be the only day that many non-observant Jews attend synagogue.[10] Yom Kippur is described in the Torah: "This shall be to you a law for all time: In the seventh month, on the tenth day of the month, you shall practice self-denial; and you shall do no manner of work, neither the citizen nor the alien who resides among you. For on this day atonement shall be made for you to cleanse you of all your sins; you shall be clean before the Lord." (Lev 16:30-31) This day is a celebration of the individual's redemption before God. It is a solemn day to be spent in prayer and inner reflection. Jews are expected to shift their minds from worldly concerns to spiritual ones. There are five restrictions that point to the five worldly concerns to be abandoned: fasting, not washing one's body, not using lotions or perfumes, not wearing leather shoes, and abstaining from sexual relations. Food, bathing, sex, possessions, and pleasures all have their place in society, but one is reminded on Yom Kippur that life is more than just these things. At night, there is an evening service at the synagogue where the Jewish community come together to humbly ask for God's forgiveness. With a clean soul, Jews start a fresh new year, and can now look forward to the future with all its possibilities.

It is no coincidence then that only four days after Yom Kippur, the joyful holiday of Succoth is celebrated. This holiday is an agricultural one. It is a time to rejoice in collecting the summer crops, and having a thankful attitude that God provides food. The symbolism of this day though is more than just agriculturally induced. This holiday is also a time to look to God as the ultimate protector of humanity. Jews are asked to leave the security of their homes and dwell in a Succoth (temporary shelter) for seven days. This is done to remind them that their homes do not provide their safety, but God does. Living in a Succoth is also an aid to remember that the Israelites dwelled in similar booths during their exodus from Egypt. It was God who is given the credit for bringing the Israelites across the dessert. He was with them on their journey in the form of a cloud. (Ex 13:21) The point is not just to reflect on this event as something that happened in the past, but to keep in mind that God is still actively protecting and guiding his people today.

The next important festival for the Jews is Pesach, or more commonly known as Passover. The central event of this festival is recalling the story of the Exodus from Egypt. This was the liberation of the Israelites from slavery which lead them into the desert for forty years of wandering in the wilderness. This journey happily ended with a victory in Canaan. It is in this new land that the Israelites built their own free nation. Pesach, then, is the celebration of the birthday of the Jewish people. The most important ritual is the Seder, a banquet during which the events of the exodus are read to everyone present. This is done to fulfill the command specifically laid out in the Tanakh, "That you may recount in the hearing of your sons and of you son's sons how I made a mockery of Egyptians and how I displayed My signs among them—in order that you may know that I am the Lord." (Ex 10:2) Unleavened bread is the main symbol of this feast. It is eaten as a reminder that the original Israelites left Egypt quickly and did not have time to let their dough rise. Unleavened bread is called Matzah, and it represents a "bread of affliction," the bread of poor and humble people.[11] More than any other group, the Jews have been an afflicted people. Through all their tribulations they have held strong to their covenant with God and looked forward to the messianic age.

The covenant would be worthless without the revelation of the Law. It is the Shavuot holiday that looks to the keystone of all Judaism—the giving of the Law. How could humanity live up to God's expectations unless they had some kind of a guideline? The Law is the central element that connects humans to God within a covenant. Studying the scriptures is a key aspect in understanding and learning the Law. Therefore, Shavuot revolves around religious education. Some traditional Jews have an all-night study session beginning the evening before the holiday. In this way, they prepare themselves for receiving the Torah on Shavuot. This holiday has also been a traditional time when many conservative and orthodox Hebrew high schools celebrate their graduation.[12]

The Jewish faith revolves around living within a covenant with God. This covenant is based on observing God's revealed commandments. These focus not only on morality but also include Jewish rituals and festivals. It is within the Jewish festivals each year that the Jews are reminded about the important themes of Creation, redemption, and revelation. These are the key elements of a living God that is active in the world. The Tanakh shows a God that is invested in his Creation. According to the scripture, when humans turned their backs on God, he did not give up on them but continued his mission to reach people and turn their hearts toward him. One way that God connected with humanity was through revelation. The prophets in the Tanakh were never shown as people searching for God; rather just the opposite, it portrays a God trying to seek out humanity. God was successful in communicating his Laws to the Jews. This Law gave them the necessary tool to aid God in the redemption of their nation, as well as the world. An important part of being a Jew is to look forward to the messianic age of peace for everyone.

BIBLIOGRAPHY

1. Cohen, Abraham. *Everyman's Talmud.* New York: Schocken Books, 1975. p. 88

2. Dosick, Rabbi Wayne. *Living Judaism, The Complete Guide to Jewish Belief, Tradition, and Practice.* New York: Harper SanFrancisco, 1995. p. 177

3. Cohen, p. 92

4. Cohen, p. XXXV

5. Dimont, Max I. *Jews, God, and History.* New York: New American Library, 1994. p. 109

6. Ibid., p. 105

7. Kaplan, Aryeh. *Sabbath Day of Eternity.* New York: National Conference of Synagogue Youth/Union of Orthodox Jewish Congregations of America, 1984. p. 7

8. Ibid., p. 21

9. Ibid., p. 23-24

10. Robinson, George. *Essential Judaism.* New York: Pocket Books, 2000. p. 97

11. Ibid., p. 120

12. Ibid., p. 127-128

CHAPTER 3:
ISLAM — GOD IS THE SINGLE CREATOR

God purposely sculpted the heavens and the earth. From his imagination, he scattered vegetation and every imaginable creature upon the world. It was God alone who breathed life into his beloved humans. There is only one source of all Creation; for to think otherwise, would mean a variety of gods ruled in heaven and that would lead to competition, arguing, grappling for top positions, and ultimately chaos. The world though, is not chaotic, but fashioned in an orderly manner. Nature obeys only one master and in a similar way, the Muslims believe people too should look to the one God for their purpose in life. Above all the oneness of God means that a Muslim must submit themselves to no one else or nothing else except for God;

for God is their Creator and because of that they owe him their entire lives.

"There is no God but God." This is the first part of a Muslim's mandatory affirmation, which quickly gets to the very heart of the Islamic faith. It is a tool to remember their eternal truth of the oneness of God. To divide God into pieces and make him more than one destroys the very essence of God. God's oneness stands at the center of his personality. He is beyond anything humans can conceive or imagine. He is the only absolute, infinite, all-mighty, and he is beyond comparison.

The second part to the Muslim's testimony of faith proclaims that as a prophet, "Muhammad is the messenger of God." Muslims believe, similar to Judaism, that God reveals himself to special people called prophets, who then in turn are responsible for giving the information to the community. In fact, Muslim's honor many of the same prophets as the Jews. Their sacred literature includes such people as Noah, Abraham, Ishmael, Isaac, Jacob, Joseph, Moses, Elijah, John, and even Jesus from Christianity. The oneness of God, to the Muslim, points to God's single message to the prophets. In other words, what was communicated to Noah was the same as that given to Joseph, to Moses, to Jesus, and finally to Muhammad. Muslim's scripture explains that, "He has revealed to you the Scripture with truth, confirming that which was revealed before it, even as He revealed the Torah and the Gospel." (Q 3:3) If these appear to be different it is because the information has been distorted over time. To Muhammad is bestowed the special honor of the seal of the prophets because his is the final and complete message uncorrupted by time.

Mecca is the lucky city that gave birth to Prophet Muhammad. It is nestled in a valley of mountains about eighty miles west of the Red Sea, in Saudi Arabia. Mecca is a rare place where the normal veil between God and earth is stretched thinner than usual, and those spiritually inclined may hear faint whispers from a mystical world beyond. The story surrounding Mecca is as old as the Bible. Abraham is the key figure; he is special because in a world filled with pagans, he still prayed to the one and only God. The Bible tells us that he had two sons both destined to the start great nations. Ishmael was born first to Abraham's slave Hagar. Later Sarah, Abraham's wife, gave birth to her own son, Isaac. Now secure with her own son, Sarah's jealousy compelled her to urge Abraham to expel Hagar and Ishmael from the household. Out on her own with very little food and water, Hagar struggled to keep her boy alive. Finally, she could bear it no more, and gently laid her son down. Sitting opposite him, she cried out in desperation, "I don't want to watch the boy die." (Gen 21:16) As she heard her son crying, she must have wept tears of sorrow as well, but God heard the boy too. It was then that "God opened Hagar's eyes, and she saw a well full of water." (Gen 21:19) Muslim's call this well Zamzam, and it is located in the sacred city of Mecca. Eventually, a sanctuary called the Ka'ba was built next to the well. Muslims believe that it was Abraham himself who established the Ka'ba. The Qur'an tells Muslims, "The first sanctuary ever built for mankind was at Bakka (Mecca), a blessed place, a guidance to the peoples ." (Q 3:96) The Arab Nation that grew around the Ka'ba is considered, by the Muslims, to be descendents of Ishmael.

Fast forwarding to the 5th century in Mecca, things had spun out of control for this city. The Abraham religion had almost disappeared, there were only a few left who were pushed to the outskirts of society where they were barely tolerated because of their rigid views.[1] The Quraysh tribe controlled Mecca. The leaders of this tribe were more focused on commercial development then morality or religion.[2] The Ka'ba was still at the center of Mecca, but it no longer stood for the one true God of Abraham and Ishmael. It had become a magnet attracting pilgrims from the surrounding tribes. The various tribes brought their own idols which they placed all around the Ka'ba, and eventually the Moabite idol of Hubal was placed in a position of honor inside the Ka'ba. The annual pilgrimage to the Ka'ba elevated the city of Mecca to the center of Arabian life. The Quraysh leaders gained both prestige and wealth because of it. For this reason, the idols were accepted and indulging the pilgrims was encouraged so that Mecca could reap the benefits.[3]

Muhammad was born into the Quraysh tribe. Early in life he suffered the loss of both his parents. He had a few years with his grandfather, who was the main caretaker of the Ka'ba. When his grandfather died, Muhammad's uncle adopted him. At the same time, his uncle also inherited the position of primary custodian of the Ka'ba. As a young boy, Muhammad spent a lot of time around the Ka'ba watching people bow to the idols therein. He was also aware of the businessmen who made and sold the statues for profit. These experiences surely had an impact on the young Muhammad.[4]

From an early age, Muhammad had earned the title "Muhammad the truthful, the trustworthy."[5] He grew up to be a strong willed and righteous man. He was also deeply spiritual, and often went to a secluded cave outside of Mecca to mediate and pray. It was during one of these normal visits to the cave that Muhammad was touched by God in a special way that took his life in a whole new direction. Muhammad was forty when the angel first appeared to him. "Recite!" He ordered Muhammad. "I am not a reciter," Muhammad replied. But the angel was adamant.[6]

Initially, the only person Muhammad confided in about his unusual experience was his wife. But God had bigger plans for him and continued to pursue Muhammad further. He soon had another revelation. "Warn your tribe of near kindred." (Q 26:214) After that, he converted some of his family.[7] His relatives helped him bravely speak out to all the people of Mecca against the polytheism that surrounded them. Many accepted his message and turned their backs on all the other gods that had become a normal part of Meccan life. His followers agreed to worship only one, all-powerful God, Allah, and gave Muhammad the title of prophet.

His revelations were memorized by his followers, and later gathered together into a book called the Qur'an. The contents of the Qur'an were revealed to Muhammad little by little throughout his life. It is the one scripture that unifies all Muslims. When read out loud it has its own rhythm, its own divine sound, which Muslim's believe add to its authority as the exact words of God. The Qur'an educates the Muslim's on a broad range of subjects including legal, moral, social, economic, philosophical, and scientific issues. The Muslim's consider it a reference for life, and they value the book because it contains God's guidance that has the capacity to lead them to heaven. The Qur'an tells Muslims "We have sent down to you the Book as an exposition of things, a guidance, a mercy and glad tiding to the Muslims." (Q 16:89)

Muhammad's main message of the Qur'an—devotion to a single God—hit a nerve with the pilgrims who brought their various idols to Mecca. The leaders of the Quraysh tribe, who were shrewd business men, were infuriated with Muhammad. His message could destroy their prestige and financial situation. At first, these leaders jeered and taunted the Muslims but as the Muslim community grew, so did the hatred against them. It escalated into violence and Muslims were forced to either flee or endure torture. They escaped to Medina which became their new home.

In Medina, Muhammad continued to receive revelations. During that time, many of the Medinese were encompassed into the fold of Islam and the prophet gained prestige in his new home. Eventually he became the leader of Medina. He formed a new government in Medina. It was based on the Islamic community held together by their belief in one God, rather than the old tribal ways of right made might.[8] Muhammad became the main arbiter when disputes arose and in this way he began the Islamic Law, (Shari'ah Law) some of his decisions were recorded in the Qur'an.

Even though the Muslims left Mecca, this did not end their problems with the Meccan Quraysh tribe. The battles raged between the two, and the Muslims ended up at war. It wasn't until several years later that Muhammad conquered Mecca and reestablished the Ka'ba as the sanctuary for Allah alone. All the idols were destroyed, and the Ka'ba became an important place of worship for the Muslims.

Due to Muhammad's earlier experiences in Mecca, he believed that humans had a natural weakness for sliding back into polytheism. In Islam, this is considered the worst sin imaginable and is given the name "*shirk*." There are two different aspects of *shirk*. First, *shirk* is diminishing God's power by adding celestial partners to him, but it could also mean taking earthly possessions or people as more important than God. If the problem is the fragmentation of God into pieces, then the solution is to focus on God's oneness. Muhammad's core message, the eternal truth of Islam, was not lost after Muhammad's death in 632 CE. *Tawhid*, the Arabic word for oneness, became the foundation on which Muslims built their religion.

The Muslims came to organize *Tawhid*, the unity of God, into three different categories. The first and most important aspect of *Tawhid* is called "unity of divine Lordship." This simply means that Allah stands alone as the only force in the universe. This type of *Tawhid* reminds Muslims that since there is only one God, then God alone is the Creator of everything.[9] The Qur'an repeatedly points Muslims to Creation for an understanding of God. "Allah created the heavens and earth with truth. Behold, therein is indeed a sign for believers." (Q 29:44) Muslims are called to use their intellect to see that God has revealed his awesome power in Creation. One can only get a grasp at how much more majestic God is than humans, when they open their eyes to the magnitude of the universe that God created. We live on a planet, in a solar system, which lies in a galaxy called the Milky Way. One of our most advanced telescopes "the Hubble Space Telescope has found there may be 125 billion galaxies in the universe."[10] Our own sun, which gives us the gifts of light, warmth, and solar power, is not even the biggest or hottest star in our galaxy. The earth itself was made perfectly for human habitat. God also created humans; every single person of the billions that occupy the earth has been made in a unique way with their own distinguishing fingerprint to prove it. We were made with joints, muscles, and bones designed to give us maximum movement. Our nervous, cardiovascular, and digestive systems were made to regulate our body and keep us healthy. And yet we sometimes forget the interconnectedness of everything. When you get down to the microscopic view of the world as protons, neutrons, and electrons that make up the atoms, those same particles that flow through our bodies and give us life also fill the entire universe. The whole of it is mind-boggling.

In the face of such a powerful, single God, the Muslim's automatic response is one of submission. This submission, however, is actually a recognition that it is only through living in harmony with God and his ways that humans can experience true freedom. Living in this way, Muslims are no longer slaves to the perceptions of others or to their own human egos. It is only God's opinion that truly counts, and this helps them bring to focus what is really important in life. For Muslims, this concept is expressed in the next form of *Tawhid* called "Unity of Worship." In this *Tawhid*, the focus shifts from who God is, to how humans should behave. "Unity of Worship" commands Muslims to worship, or submit, to God and nothing else. This includes not just other false gods, but also placing people or things above God. Worship means more than just praising God, but really encompasses devoting one's entire life to God first, above all else.

For Muslims, the appropriate way to submit to God is to follow the Shari'ah Law. Recall that this had it's beginnings in Medina with the prophet and the Qur'an. After Muhammad died, under new leadership, the Muslims tried to keep the Law based on the overall views held in the Qur'an, but in some cases this proved to be very difficult. As time went on, the Sunnah and Hadith developed to aid in producing new laws. The Sunnah is the traditions and a specific way of life that the prophet Muhammad modeled during his lifetime. The Hadiths are the prophet's sayings that were not recorded in the Qur'an, but yet still memorized by his close companions. With the Qur'an in the lead position and the Sunnah and Hadith working in cooperation with it, the Law was created based as closely as possible on the teachings of the prophet.

The Shari'ah Law spells out clearly for those who take heed how God expects Muslims to behave toward him and others. It details the straight path. It is simplified so that all can follow it. In the law, every major action is classified in relation to how God would feel about that act. Behaviors that deeply offend God are deemed forbidden. Other behaviors that are not as disgusting as the forbidden ones, yet still reprehensible, are called abominable and Muslims should avoid these acts. In the center of the spectrum, for the Law, are permissible actions which God is indifferent to. On the opposite side, are things that cause God to look more favorably on the Muslim; these are recommended actions. Lastly, is the obligatory category, and these are actions that God expects a Muslim to perform.[11] The obligatory actions are needed in order to live an appropriate life directed towards God's purpose. In other words, they nourish Muslims spiritually and are good for the whole community.

The category of obligatory actions includes the five pillars of wisdom. These are the outward signs that point to the inner love and devotion to God. Having a wonderful spiritual feeling is great, but if it is only confined within an individual's heart and moves no further, then what good is it? The importance of actions is summed up by Imam Ali, who was not only the prophet's cousin, but also the 4th Caliph (leader) as well.

> Islam is submission, submission is conviction, conviction is affirmation, affirmation is acknowledgement, acknowledgement is performance of obligations, and performance of obligations is good deeds.[12]

Basically, if one is a true Muslim, then submission to God should lead him or her to doing good deeds. The five pillars are only the basic building blocks that are an inspirational boost toward even greater righteousness. They also help to define exactly what it means to be a Muslim.

The first of the pillars is prayer. Out of all the pillars, this one stands out because it is repeated daily and requires the greatest perseverance; however, it also grants the best rewards as well. Muslims believe that prayer is a ladder that leads straight to God. One Hadith reminds Muslims that "Prayer is the ascension of the faithful."[13] Muslims are expected to pray five times a day. The first prayer should be done before sunrise. This early dawn prayer includes a recitation of the first chapter of the Qur'an. It reads:

> In the name of Allah, the compassionate, the Merciful. Praise be to Allah, the Lord of the Worlds; The Compassionate, the Merciful; master of the Day of Judgment; You alone do we worship, and to you alone we pray for help; Guide us to the Straight path: The way of those whom You have favoured: Not of those who have incurred Your wrath. Nor of those who go astray. (Q 1:1-7)

Everyday a Muslim is expected to wake up with this prayer of praise and request for guidance on their lips. It is a reminder to them that this day should be lived for God. The next prayer is to be done around noon, a third prayer in the afternoon, another just after sunset, and the last prayer can be done anytime before midnight. These prayers must be learned and memorized as there is a certain procedure that must be performed for the prayers to be done properly. The essence of Muslim prayers dives deep into the creation of a person as both body and soul. Their prayers, therefore, are not just for the body or the soul individually, but incorporate both. This is done by the physical movement of their body during prayers and reciting verses from the Qur'an that affects them spiritually. It intermingles the body and spirit making them one and connecting them both to the divine.[14] Not only does prayer connect a Muslim's body and soul to God, but it also connects the Muslims to each other. Every Friday, Muslims are encouraged to go to their local Mosque to come together as a community to pray. At this time, there is also a sermon from the local Iman at the Mosque.

The next important pillar of faith is fasting. Believers can fast any time during the year in order to purify themselves. But the required fast is done in the Islamic month of Ramadan. For this entire month, Muslims are asked to refrain from eating, drinking, and sexual contact from sunrise to sunset. Most of the prophets, sages, and mystics throughout history have used fasting as a way to overcome their base self. Not only does fasting clear the body and mind, but it reminds Muslims of what poor people experience on a daily bases. Muhammad expressed the importance of this pillar when he proclaimed, "Hunger is the food of God."[15] This pillar is associated with a Muslim's festival day called *Eid-ul-Fitr*, celebrating the end of the fast. On this day, Muslim's assemble together to pray and later enjoy a feast with their families.

A pilgrimage, or hajj, is also a required as an act of faith; this is for those who are able, of course. This is not just a tourist vacation to the Mecca, but rather involves a series of important rituals. It all begins with the proper clothing for the pilgrimage. Pilgrims are expected to wear white, seamless robes, men cannot shave, and women are not allowed jewelry. In this way, no one stands out as wealthy, or poor, and all appear equal as God's Creations. When dressing into the proper attire, a prayer must be said, "I am here, O Lord, I am here!" followed by, "You, who have no partner—I am here! Surely all praise and blessings are Yours, and the Kingdom—I am here, O Lord, I am here."[16] The main focus of the pilgrimage is the house of God—the Ka'ba—it is a symbol of God's oneness. Pilgrims circle around the house seven times, which reminds them to embrace God as the center of their life. Another ritual is racing between the two small hills called Safa and Marwa. This rite recalls Hagar's desperate search for water, and God's miraculous spring of saving water, the Zamzam. The essential ritual to complete the hajj spans a whole day, which is called Arafat Day. This day receives its name from Mount Arafat which is special because it is the place where Prophet Muhammad delivered his farewell speech. Pilgrims, still dressed in white, spend the day standing on or near Mount Arafat praying and asking for God's forgiveness. Many shed tears of joy during this time, as they are relieved from the burden of sin. On the following day, the atmosphere changes from somber to joyous as the pilgrims rejoice in God's mercy. Muslims everywhere celebrate this day as a major Islamic festival called *Eid Ul-Adha*. Muslims are expected to sacrifice an animal (cow, goat, or sheep) and eat it. A generous portion of the sacrifice must also be shared with the poor. This tradition relates back to the time of Abraham. He was given an excruciatingly difficult test from God asking him to sacrifice his own son. He passed, and God had him sacrifice a ram instead of his son. On this festival, Muslims are reminded that they need to have the same kind of devotion and trust in God as Abraham did.

Another pillar of faith for Islam is charity. Muslims are asked to give 2 ½ percent of their income to their Mosque, so that it can be distributed to those in need. This reminds Muslims that their wealth is not their own, but comes to them from God and should be shared. For one never knows when they might find themselves in a difficult situation as well.

The last pillar of Islam is actually the first and most important. All the other four pillars lead up to and encourage this first pillar, which is proclaiming the statement with a sincere heart that "There is no God but God, and Muhammad is his prophet." This completely defines who is a Muslim and who is not. If you do not believe in one God or you do not believe in Muhammad, then you cannot call yourself a Muslim.

Following the straight path as laid out by the Shari'ah Law is not always easy. It is especially difficult in today's world, where religion has a tendency to be benched to other supposedly more important things. Islam's main thrust from its beginnings has been to bring religion back to the top of a Muslim's priority list. To put God first requires a constant everyday struggle. The Qur'an reminds Muslims, "O you who believe! Be mindful of your duty to Allah, and seek the way of approach to Him, and strive in His way in order that you may succeed."(Q 5:35) Striving after God's way, against our own base desires, is called Jihad.

The Arabic word Jihad has recently received a bad reputation. Jihad is used for the majority of Muslims to describe their internal struggle, but it may also be used to explain an external one against evil as well. This kind of Jihad is only necessary when Muslims are called to fight in defense of Islam. There is one verse in the Qur'an that sums up this philosophy of war. "Fight for the sake of Allah those that who fight against you, but do not attack them first. Allah does not love the aggressors." (Q 2:190) In other words, sometimes people, nations, or religions are faced with standing up to the bullies and fighting back. It is an irony throughout history that sometimes peace can only be obtained through war. Without war, the dictators of the world would be allowed to continue their destructive paths. Where would the United

States be without first having fought the Revolutionary War? Where would our world be if the allies of WW II had not stood up to Hitler? And where would Islam be had they not confronted the Meccans?

The final aspect of *Tawhid* is the "Unity of the Divine Attributes." This part of *Tawhid* explains that God's attributes are one with his essence and in no way separates God into parts.[17] The Qur'an references ninety-nine attributes of God; these can also be referred to as his names. Though God's oneness is at the center of his personality, Islam recognizes many different aspects of God by his different names. Some of these names include the Holy, the Merciful, the Source of Peace, the Creator, the Wise, the Loving, and the Judge. Many of God's names are restricted to God alone. He is the only Creator, Judge, and the Praiseworthy. Other divine attributes of God are reflected in humans when we chose to act righteously. Some of these include the Merciful, the Source of Peace, and the Forgiving. Muslims are encouraged to learn all of God's names for two reasons. The first is that in knowing God's attributes, they can strive constantly toward imitating the ones that belong to human nature. Secondly, learning about God's names helps Muslims to more clearly comprehend who God is. Memorizing the names is a good start, but Muslims are also encouraged to work toward understanding each attribute. The Islamic faith is about action, but it is also about being sincere in those actions. The way Muslims come to have a sincere heart in all their actions is to know God, especially by remembering his oneness. They also achieve this by constantly keeping in mind all of God's blessed attributes which provides for them a full portrait of God.

Having lived a life full of meaning because a Muslim knew God, loved God, and lived for the one God, the Muslims have an eternal life with God to look forward to at the end of their time on earth. The Qur'an constantly reminds them of this. "This is the path of your Lord, a straight path. We have detailed Our revelations for a people who take heed. For them is the home of peace with their Lord. He will be their Protecting Friend because of what they used to do." (Q 6:126-127)

BIBLIOGRAPHY

1. Lings, Martin. *Muhammad, His Life Based on the Earliest Sources*. Rochester: Inner Traditions International, 1983. p. 16

2. Engineer, Asghar Ali. *The Origin and Development of Islam*. London: Sangam Books, 1987, p. 38

3. Lings, p. 15

4. Gabriel, Mark A., PhD. *Jesus and Muhammad, Profound Differences and Surprising Similarities*. Lake Mary, FL: Charisma House, 2004. p. 27

5. Al-Qazwini, Moustafa. *Discovering Islam*. Costa Mesa, CA: The Islamic Educational Center of Orange County, 2001. p. 24

6. Lings, p. 43-44

7. Lings, p. 50

8. Engineer, p. 93

9. Abdul-Rahman, Muhammad Saed. *Islam: Questions and Answers, Divine Unity (Tawheed)*. London: MSA Publication Limited, 2003. p. 6

10. NASA'S Imagine the Universe Website. Topic—Milky Way and other galaxies. November 27, 2002. <htt://www.Imagine.gsfc.nasa.gov.docs/ask_astro/answers/021127a.html>

11. Nasr, Seyyed Hossein. *The Heart of Islam, Enduring Values for Humanity*, New York: HarperSanFrancisco, 2002. p. 126

12. Al-Qazwini, p. 4

13. Bayman, Henry. *The Secret of Islam, Love and Law in the Religion of Ethics*. Berkeley: North Atlantic Books, 2003. p. 77

14. Ibid., p. 77-78

BIBLIOGRAPHY

15. Ibid., p. 212
16. Al-Qazwini, p. 79-80
17. Abdul-Rahman, p. 8-9

CHAPTER 4:
CHRISTIANITY—GOD IS LOVE

Instinctively, most people feel they have to work at being accepted or loved. Women spend money and time on their appearance in order to win a man's heart. Men think they have to drive expensive sports cars or have a successful job to deserve a good woman. Even when it comes to God, most people typically think they have to do something to win God's love. Christianity has a startling truth that turns this theory upside down; it's called "grace." In a nutshell, grace means "God is love." (1 Jn 4:16) Philip Yancey, a Christian writer, explains that, "God's grace means there is nothing we can do to make God love us more, . . . and it means there is nothing we can do to make God love us less. . . . God already loves us as much as an infinite God can possibly love.",[1] The idea of God's grace also incorporates a tangible touch of receiving God's awesome love. For those buried under the weight of their own sins, God offers forgiveness and release of guilt. For others struggling through a difficult situation, God has wisdom and strength available. For depressed or lonely people, he offers support. Whatever a person needs God has a gift to make them whole again. The fact that God loves humanity and wants to freely give humans everything they need for spiritual fulfillment, including and most importantly eternal salvation with him, is the Christian answer to the question "Who is God?"

All Christians are combined under the banner of Christianity by a man named Jesus. The gospels give Christians very little information about Jesus' early life. It is known that he was born about 2000 years ago to a poor family. Two of the gospels, Matthew and Luke, inform Christians that Jesus was born of a virgin named Mary. I'm sure that the people in his hometown had a hard time accepting that news. He was probably labeled a bastard. As if that wasn't bad enough, he lived in the town of Nazareth that was scoffed at by more pious Jews. One quote from the gospel of John makes this point, "'Nazareth!' exclaimed Nathanael. 'Can anything good come from Nazareth?'" (Jn 1:46) From his lowly beginnings, he broke away from his family and began a life of ministry. He gained popularity quickly. His miracles got him noticed, but what kept faithful followers interested was his personal charisma that inspired people to live better lives.

The message of Jesus was empowering. In a world taut with political tensions, racism, and sexism he lovingly taught about the grace of God. Many might disagree with that statement, as the word grace is almost completely absent from all four gospels. Jesus, though, did not preach about grace from a pulpit; instead, he walked among the common people using parables to convey his message of grace. To Jesus, the grace of God seeks and retrieves a lost one. This is portrayed in the parable of the good shepherd who goes after the one lost sheep and carefully places it on his shoulders and carries it home. (Luke 15:3-7) The grace of God encourages and gives plenty of opportunity for growth toward righteousness. This is seen in the parable of the fig tree. The owner of the tree wants to cut it down because it has not bore fruit yet, but the gardener responds, "Sir, give it one more chance. Leave it another year, and I'll give it special attention and plenty of fertilizer. If we get figs next year, fine. If not, then you can cut it down." (Luke 13:8-9) These parables not only reveal something about God but also about humans. The parables present a graceful God, but they also show that humans need God's grace. Without the grace of God, people are like lost sheep or barren fig trees.

"So if you sinful people know how to give good gifts to your children, how much more will your heavenly Father give good gifts to those who ask him." (Matt 7:11) Jesus taught about a loving and giving God, in other words, a graceful God. He does not, though, ever use the actual word grace; instead his focus is on the "kingdom of God." This "kingdom of God" that Jesus spoke about is the product of a world filled with God's grace. Jesus saw himself as the initiator of the new kingdom. According to the Gospel of Mark, in the beginning of Jesus' ministry he proclaimed, "'The time promised by God has come at last.' He announced, 'The kingdom of God is near! Repent of your sins and believe the good News!'" (Mark 1:15) The time had come for a new order and a new way of thinking and being, and Jesus himself was to instigate it; but only the grace of God would bring it to fulfillment. Grace, for Jesus, was like a seed that grows in an individual's heart and when it comes to fruition, it gives people the power to become righteous. As this happens, then the world moves closer to the realization of the "kingdom of God."

He used many analogies and parables to illustrate this point. In one case, he compared the kingdom of God to a mustard seed. "The kingdom of heaven is like a mustard seed planted in a field. It is the smallest of all seeds, but it becomes the largest of garden plants; it grows into a tree, and the birds come and make nests in its branches." (Matt 13:31-32) Another analogy illustrates this point, "What else is the kingdom of God like? It is like the yeast a woman used in making bread. Even though she put only a little yeast in three measures of flour, it permeated every part of the dough." (Luke 13:20-21) Here, the flour is like God's word as Jesus taught it, and the yeast can be compared to the grace of God that was also needed to make the final product of leavened bread. Finally, the parable of the "sower" also shows the same thing.

Listen! A farmer went out to plant some seeds. As he scattered them across his field, some seeds fell on a footpath, and the birds came and ate them. Other seeds fell on shallow soil with underlying rock. The seeds sprouted quickly because the soil was shallow. But the plants soon wilted under the hot sun, and since they didn't have deep roots they died. Other seeds fell among thorns that grew up and choked out the tender plants. Still other seeds fell on fertile soil, and they produced a crop that was thirty, sixty and even a hundred times as much as had been planted! (Matt 13:3-9)

The explanation of this parable is in Matthew 13:18-23, but basically the seed sown on the path, the rocky places, and among the thorns are like people who have heard the word and received it, but for various reasons it did not last and eventually got lost and forgotten. The seed sown on rich soil, however, represents those who heard the word, understood it, and applied it to their lives. These were the people who opened their hearts to God's grace allowing them to work with God's plan.

While Jesus was alive, the disciples had the expectation that his kingdom was political. They believed that he would eventually overthrow the Roman government and place himself in the seat of King of Israel. Their vision of Jesus was influenced by the Hebrew Scriptures which portrays the Messiah as a "king who rules with wisdom. He will do what is just and right throughout the land. And this will be his name: 'The Lord Is Our Righteousness.' In that day Judah will be saved, and Israel will live in safety." (Jer 23:5-6) Jesus probably did perceive himself as the prophesized Messiah. When questioned by followers of John as to whether he was the expected one, Jesus replied, "Go back to John and tell him what you have seen and heard—the blind see, the lame walk, the lepers are cured, the deaf hear, the dead are raised to life, and the Good News is being preached to the poor." (Luke 7:22) This is a reference to what the Prophet Isaiah said about the arrival of the Messiah. "He is coming to save you. And when he comes, he will open the eyes of the blind and unplug the ears of the deaf. The lame will leap like a deer, and those who cannot speak will sing for joy!" (Is 35:4-6) Isaiah also proclaimed that "In that day you will sing: 'I will praise you, O Lord! You were angry with me, but not any more. Now you comfort me. See, God has come to save me. I will trust in him and not be afraid. The Lord God is my strength and my song; he has given me victory.'" (Is 12:1-2) To most Jews, this statement meant that Judah would have victory over her aggressors. This is the new kingdom of Israel that the disciples were hopeful for. Jesus, however, had a different interpretation. The comfort and strength would come from grace, which would give people victory over their sins. The kingdom that Jesus was inaugurating was never political, but a spiritual kingdom sown with grace.

Jesus saw his main purpose as a doctor who came to heal the sick—the sinners. The cure was grace. Jesus reached out to people and offered grace, and through his teachings, his compassion, and his miracles many people were transformed and their hearts turned towards goodness. His ministry, however, with its focus on the spiritual rather than the Law, led him into direct conflict with both the religious and political leaders of the day. He purposely chose not fight his enemies, but freely gave his body over to them. When Jesus died, his disciples must have been overwhelmed with a feeling of despair, figuring that the world was filled with evil and it was futile to continue to fight against it. On the third day after Jesus' death, however, he restored hope to his followers by miraculously rising from the dead. This event was a clear sign that in the end, grace has power over sin.

Whether the resurrection was a historical event is irrelevant. The fact is that soon after Jesus' death something sparked a change in the lives of his followers. The disciples stopped hiding and burst into the world spreading with great joy the good news of the gospel of Jesus. This was the birth of Christianity. The strength, energy, and wisdom that they gained after the resurrection eventually came to be understood as the workings of the Holy Spirit. After the disciples had received these powerful gifts of the Holy Spirit, they remembered that Jesus himself had spoken about sending it to them. "And I will ask the Father and he will give you another Advocate, who will never leave you. He is the Holy Spirit, who leads into all truth." (Jn 14:16-17) This is a key concept of Christianity. The grace of God is given to Christians through the Holy Spirit, which is sent by God.

Christians feel blessed because they do not have to wait until they get to heaven to feel God's fondness for them. The Holy Spirit resides in their hearts where from the inside out it can warm the whole body to the presence of God's love. Functioning from the inner depths of a person, the Spirit is a powerful, guiding force helping Christians turn toward righteousness. The Spirit is also important to Christians because working through the individual lives of Christians he has the power to drive the direction of the Christian church. On a more global scale, the Spirit will skillfully lead the world toward the actualization of the "kingdom of God" that Jesus described while he was on earth.

The Holy Spirit from the beginning of Christianity was connected to the idea of baptism. All Christians are baptized, following the example of Jesus himself. Every gospel account shows that through baptism, the spirit of God came upon Jesus. He was baptized by John the Baptist who was "in the wilderness and preached that people should be baptized to show that they had repented of their sins and turned to God to be forgiven." (Mark 1:4) Simply then, baptism is a way for Christians to publicly announce that they want to repent from their sins and accept the Holy Spirit. This is clear in the book of Acts which tells us that on Pentecost, Peter stood up to a large crowd and said, "Repent of your sins and turn to God, and be baptized in the name of Jesus Christ for the forgiveness of your sins. Then you will receive the gift of the Holy Spirit." (Acts 2:38) Baptism is the one deciding factor on who is and is not a Christian. If a person is not baptized by the time they are an adult, then they are certainly not a Christian. For Christians, baptism holds their eternal truth, that through God's grace they will have eternal life.

Both Jesus and the Holy Spirit eventually came to be understood as part of the One True God. This idea developed theologically into the trinity. The trinity is the special way that Christians have a relationship with God. They understand him to be made up of three persons, but at the same time only one God. At first, this seems puzzling, and Christians have no real explanation for this mathematical anomaly. Basically, it comes down to being a mystery from God. But if you ponder the idea of three, many things come to mind. For example, the three parts of life are space, matter, and time. Yet each of these can be broken into three factions as well. Take space; it is three-dimensional length, width, and height. Matter as well has three different manifestations—solid, liquid, and gas. Time can be broken into the past, present, and future. Even with humans—most religions would agree—are made up of three parts: a body, soul, and spirit. Three appears to be some mystical number that has meaning in the universe. So in an odd way, it seems only logical that the divine should have three parts as well Christianity defines these aspects of God as Father, Son, and Holy Spirit.

The God that created the world as described in Genesis and also revealed himself to Abraham, Isaac, and Jacob is the same Father that Jesus spoke of in the New Testament Gospels. The Father's personality is thoroughly described in the Hebrew Scriptures. In those writings, he is portrayed as the most powerful being and at the same time full of compassion and mercy for the humans he created. The Christians agree with the Jews, that the Father delivered the Law to Moses. Jesus saw his purpose as not to abolish the Law, but to fulfill it. (Matt 5:17) For the Christians, the Hebrew Scriptures (which they renamed the Old Testament) are the background which leads up to Jesus. In addition to everything the Old Testament proclaims about the Father, the Christians also believe that he, out of devotion for humans, sent both Jesus and later the Holy Spirit to continuously help humans overcome sin.

Jesus has always been the center of Christianity. The Christian faith is named such after Christ, meaning Messiah. The two most important Christian holidays—Christmas and Easter—represent his arrival and departure from the world. Christmas is the commemoration of Jesus' birthday. One tradition on this holiday is to put up Christmas lights; this is done to remember that Jesus is the light of the world. Christians also place nativity scenes in their homes to be reminded of Jesus' humble beginnings of being born in a stable. Easter is the glorious celebration of Jesus rising from the dead and returning to heaven. His resurrection is an assurance that Christians will also rise to heaven as well. The theme for this holiday is new life; it is reflected in bright colors, chicks, and Easter eggs.

Though Jesus is the key figure, it is, however, through the eyes of St. Paul that the idea of grace and sin became solidified. It is actually St. Paul's letters to the various churches that forms most of the New Testament. His letters gave leadership and direction to the budding, new religion. In fact, Paul's letters are the first documentation from the early Christian days. Many see the gospels first in the New Testament and assume they were written first, but actually, Paul's letters were penned before the gospels during the 50s and early 60s CE, where the gospels were written later between 70 CE and 100 CE.

Paul was born about the same time as Jesus, but they never actually knew each other. Paul and Jesus were almost complete opposites. Where Jesus belonged to a poor family in Galilee, Paul was born to a privileged one in Tarsus, a metropolis seaport. While Jesus probably spoke the common language of Aramaic, Paul, on the other hand, spoke the scholarly language of Greek. Jesus portrayed a lot of self-confidence, whereas Paul had a tendency toward self-negativity. A glimpse of this is noticeable in his writings. Paul gives away his own sense of guilt and overburden with sin with his cry, "Oh what a miserable person that I am! Who will free me from this life that is dominated by sin and death?" (Rom 7:24) and again, "The trouble is with me, for I am all too human, a slave to sin. I don't really understand myself, for I want to do what is right, but I don't do it, Instead, I do what I hate." (Rom 7:14-15)

It is well known that Paul used to be Saul who persecuted the early Christians; this may be where his guilt stems from. One can only speculate today, but the important fact still remains that Paul had a real need to free himself from his overwhelming sense of guilt. Paul gained that freedom on the road to Damascus when he encountered a vision of the risen Christ. He had experienced God's gift of forgiveness and unconditional love that was so powerful that it changed his life. He gave up being Saul the tormentor of Christians to become Paul the apostle on a mission to spread the Christian gospel of grace. These feeling were so passionate that they fueled his missionary work, even though he had to endure imprisonment and beatings. None of that mattered, because he was forgiven and loved. Paul attributed all of this to God's grace, and for this reason it became the most important theological idea in Christianity.

To Paul, the theory of grace implied the opposite as well, that the world was filled with sin. It was Paul that espoused that we are all sinners. "When Adam sinned, sin entered the world. Adam's sin brought death, so death spread to everyone, for everyone sinned." (Rom 5:12) This established the entire framework from which Christianity was formed. Not all Christians take the story of Adam and Eve as a literal event in history, but they do agree that symbolically or literally this story explains how sin entered the world. For Christians, if grace is the answer then sin is the problem, and it plagues everyone. Paul tells them, "For everyone has sinned; we all fall short of God's glorious standard." (Rom 3:23).

For this message, Christians have been criticized as being too focused on the negative aspect of humans—their sinfulness. Their attackers say that this causes guilt and lack of self-worth in the followers of Christianity. Yet in taking a real look at the world, it is easy to see that this doctrine of sin is correct. Murder, molestation, kidnappings, robberies, and assaults of every kind are still prevalent throughout the world. But some might argue, "I am not as bad as people who do those horrible things." There is also lying, cheating, gossiping, adultery, greed, and coveting what others have. These may seem small in comparison, but Jesus saw them as the beginnings of a slippery slope toward the bigger sins. Jesus warned Christians, "Anyone who even looks at a woman with lust has already committed adultery with her in his heart" (Matt 5:28) and "If you commit murder, you are subject to judgment. But I say, if you are even angry with someone, you are subject to judgment!" (Matt 5:21-22)

The truth is then that all humans are sinners, as Paul put down in writing during the early formation of the Christian Church. But if this was the full extent of the gospel, then what a sad and pitiful thing that would be. How could it be considered the good news as Christians refer to their gospel? The good news of the gospel is that there is a fix for our sinfulness. Paul explains the solution in his letter to the Romans. "Sin is no longer your master, for you no longer live under the requirements of the law. Instead you live under the freedom of God's grace." (Rom 6:14) Grace, the eternal truth of Christianity, is the good news of the Gospel.

The Christians believe grace is a free gift from God; therefore, it can never be earned. They also realize that it is grace that forgives sins, and so makes salvation for humans possible. This raises an important question. How do Christians receive God's grace? The answer is that the healing grace of God is abundantly available to everyone. Grace is like God's hand that is always available reaching down from heaven. All Christians have to do is grab it and hold on tight, and then he will lift them up out of their sinful natures. But in order to receive God's grace, one has to know it's available and ask for it. Jesus told the Christians, "For everyone who asks, receives. Everyone who seeks, finds. And to everyone who knocks, the door will be opened." (Matt 7:8) He is not talking here about requesting good grades or asking for a superstar date on Friday night. Jesus is certainly not equating God to Santa Clause who hands out free gifts. Instead, what Jesus is trying to convey is that if someone asks for grace, then God will give them the spiritual gifts that they need.

But not everyone seeks and values God's grace. In fact, some find it hard to deal with the whole concept of grace. To them, it seems like God lets people of the hook to easily for their sins. People want punishment for bad behavior; otherwise, they believe that justice has not occurred, especially if they were the recipient of the bad deed. The world works in the realm of our human laws. Laws are a necessary structure for our society. They, however, do not have the power to change people's hearts. In fact, sometimes laws instill feelings of rebellion against authority. Right from the start, Adam and Eve resisted the only Law God laid down. "You may freely eat the fruit of every tree in the garden—except the tree of the knowledge of good and evil. (Gen 2:16-17) So, of course, since they were forbidden the tree of knowledge that is the one that became desirable. Every one knows that the couple eventually succumbed to their craving for the fruit, and so disobeyed God. Things have not changed much since the early dawn of humanity; people still resist the law. Grace, unlike the law, understands what is in someone's heart. It sees all the circumstances in a person's life leading up to their bad decisions and transgressions. Grace forgives sin; and furthermore, it does not ask for any payment or recompense. It is God's love for humans even though we are imperfect and incapable of following his Laws. Christians believe that grace is given freely to those who accept it and repent from their sins. But our human need for justice cries, "Not fair" because if grace abounds, then that opens up a loophole for sin. Some believe that with grace, people are allowed to follow their own selfish desires only to turn around afterwards to ask for forgiveness and be welcomed back under God's protective wing of grace.

Those who see grace in this way have not really understood grace at all. For one who has been touched with God's loving grace does not return to their former life of sin. Grace has the effect of opening a person's eyes to the complete ugliness of sin. It is like seeing oneself walking through life covered in mud. Once sin's horrible nature is so clearly revealed, that person has no desire to ever return to that state. This leads to humility and dependence on God's help to stay away from sin in the future. When true humbleness and sincerity in repentance happens, only then does God's grace give people the power to conquer their sinful natures.

The theme of previously appalling sinners being transformed into excellent people of faith is a common theme in Christianity. Peter, the lead disciple, when first approached by Jesus instinctively fell to his knees and cried out, "Oh, Lord, please leave me—I'm too much of a sinner to be around you." (Luke 5:8) The gospels also show that Peter lacked the strength to stand by Jesus during his darkest hour, denying him three times. This same Peter, after the crucifixion and resurrection, went out and courageously spread the gospel. Tradition also tells us that he died a martyr in the name of Jesus. We have already mentioned Paul and his struggles against sin. After receiving God's grace, Paul went forth to become a great Christian missionary, whose letters make up most of the New Testament.

Another famous conversion was St. Augustine, a bishop from Hippo (324 -430). From a very early age, he had trouble controlling his sexual desires. In his own work *Confessions*, he describes how deeply entangled in sin he had become. "But, fool that I was, I foamed in my wickedness as the sea and, forsaking thee, followed the rushing of my own tied, and burst out of all thy bounds." (Book 2, 2:4)[2] In a climatic inner battle of the soul, Augustine finally realized that he was weak and could not control his own passions. He yearned for God to rescue him from his own selfish desires. God bestowed his grace on Augustine, and he converted to Christianity. After his conversion he proclaimed, "Thou wast with me, but I was not with thee . . . Thou didst call and cry aloud, and didst force open my deafness. Thou didst gleam and shine, and didst chase away my blindness. . . . Thou didst touch me, and I burned for thy peace." (Book 10, 27:38)[3] Three years after being a Christian, by popular demand, Augustine was ordained a priest. It was only a short time later that he became Bishop of Hippo. Augustine's writings and teachings were so imperative to the development of Western Christianity that eventually he has was given the title "Doctor of the Church."[4] Later in 1303 CE, Pope Boniface VIII canonized him into sainthood.

In a similar fashion, another conversion by grace was John Newton. Again, we see the same pattern. At first, Newton was living a life of complete sinfulness as a coarse, cruel slave trader. Once God touched his heart though, he slowly began to change. Eventually, he did a complete turn around and no longer traded slaves; instead, he joined the abolition movement against slavery.[5] It was John Newton who, in 1884, wrote the very popular Christian song *Amazing Grace*:

> Amazing grace how sweet the sound that that saved a wretch like me!
> I once was lost, but now am found, was blind but now can see.
> T'was grace that taught my heart to fear, And grace my fears relieved;
> how precious did that grace appear the hour I first believed!
> Through many dangers, toils, and snares I have already come;
> 'Tis grace has brought me safe thus far, And grace will lead me home.

This song does an excellent job of explaining the eternal truth of Christianity—GRACE.

BIBLIOGRAPHY

1. Yancey, Philip. *What's So Amazing About Grace?* Grand Rapids: Zondervan, 1997. p. 70

2. *Augustine:Confessions*. Translated and edited by Albert C. Outler, Ph.D., D.D., Book 2, Chapter 2:4

3. Ibid, Book 10, Chapter 27:38

4. Klein, Rev. Peter. *The Catholic Source Book.* Orlando: Harcourt Religion Publishers, 2000. p. 412-413 Yancey, p. 281

CHAPTER 5:
HINDUISM — GOD IS THE CONSCIOUSNESS OF ALL REALITY

Though our bodies contain many different components such as organs, muscles, bones, and blood, they all work together in unified manner so that a person can function as an individual. This is all possible because of the brain which directs and gives information to all the various parts of the body. According to the Hindus, God is the consciousness of all reality. He is the underlying connection between everything, like the brain keeping it all operating harmoniously. Within our body, the different parts have no minds of their own, and therefore have no choice but to comply with the brain's messages. People, on the other hand, can decide to be a part of God's overall plan or not. Consider if a foot rebelled and refused to walk, the entire body would be stuck. In a similar fashion, when a person believes they are independent and not part of God's reality, not only does the whole system suffer, but the individual as well. That person becomes spiritually dead and disconnected from God, like a purple and black gangrenous toe that eventually must be severed from the body. Except God is not willing to lose even a little pinky toe; he has a plan to make sure that everyone eventually gains salvation. Hindus believe that if a person becomes spiritually detached from God, then upon death their soul is reborn again in another body to continue its journey toward God. Eventually, maybe through many lifetimes, a person becomes aware of the universal mind behind all of reality and their unity with it. Once this point is reached a person is considered to be God-conscious or self-realized. This knowledge leads a person to naturally comply with God's plans, and gain eternal salvation. The term moksha is the Hindu word for salvation; it is defined as enjoying eternal bliss with God.

The Hindu religion has its beginnings in the Vedic literature. These texts are part of what holds all the various sects of Hinduism together under one religion. If a person does not accept the Vedas, they are not considered a Hindu. For this reason, these documents have been meticulously preserved over the years. The dating of these scriptures is still being debated in the scholastic circles today. The consensus, though, is that the first hymns were probably written down no earlier then 1500 BC, and the last Veda was produced before 900 BC.[1] There are four Vedas in all. They include the *Rig Veda*, the *Sama Veda*, the *Yajur Veda*, and the *Athara Veda*. The *Rig Veda* is the oldest and most important, from which the others eventually sprouted. It was produced by the Aryans who originally were tribal herdsmen who eventually settled in the northwest part of India called the Punjab.[2] It is a collection of 1028 hymns that give praise to an assortment of different gods.

This book is the initial inspirational spark of Hinduism. Though it does not contain all the tenants of the modern faith, it does provide the elementary concepts that over time would grow into a vision of God as the ultimate reality or consciousness of all things. One such idea is that of "cosmic order" or the Veda Sanskrit word "*rta*." From very early in the *Rig Veda*, the Aryans had realized that the world had a natural rhythm to it. They witnessed the seasons flowing from one to the next, night following day, and rivers winding their way to oceans. This regular process of things they decided was God's order, or also deemed God's Law. According to the hymns, the gods "spread abroad the streams by stablished law, and in the field the plants that blossom and bear seed." (RV 2.13.7) Also, the "flowing of the floods is Law, truth is the sun's extended light." (RV 1.105.12) The Law brings all the gods into unity with one another, as they all must follow the Law, and were born from the Law. The *Rig Veda* proclaims, "Even as Varuna, Mitra, Aryaman deserve: ye are the charioteers of Law. True to Law, born in Law the strengtheners of Law, terrible, haters of the false" (RV 7.66.12-13)

Initially in the *Rig Veda*, *rta* took a back seat to the sacrifice, which played the star role in the Veda. The book explains the need for sacrifice, which gods to sacrifice to, and what rewards one could gain from the activity. The sacrifice grew from its humble beginnings as a way to gain favor with the gods and receive worldly gains, into the link between God and man that kept the world from falling into chaos. By the last book in the *Rig Veda*, it was believed that the initial creation of the world was linked to the sacrifice of the primordial being, Purusha, where the different parts of his body turned into the different pieces of the universe.[3] From this, the Hindu's gathered that cosmic order was dependent on a continual reenactment of the initial sacrifice. If they failed to sacrifice, they thought the world would lose its natural order and turn into chaos. At this point, people were no longer merely enjoying the fruits of God's Creation, but had been upgraded to an essential part of the overall system of the universe.

With this bond between the sacrifice and cosmic order, the term dharma, eventually came to replace *rta*. As a key aspect of the Hindu faith, dharma, if understood fully, explains the Hindu's perception of God. Dharma includes the idea that God's natural laws preserve and bind the entire universe together, basically *rta*; but it also widens that concept to include people and their actions that bring harmony to the world.[4] Anything that people do to align with God's cosmic order is considered dharma. On the other hand, adharma is when people oppose

God's natural ways, and it brings chaos to the world. At its very basic level then, dharma is a set of laws that people should follow in order to work with God's overall cosmic plan. But, dharma is more than that; it is an internal alignment with God which enriches a person's spiritual relations with him. If God is understood as the brain that directs and gives life to all parts of the body, or universe, then dharma is being tapped into that brain. This leads a person to God-consciousness, and eventually salvation.

The complete idea of dharma evolved over time. There were three important stages during its development. Initially, the Aryan's social structure revolved around the sacrifice and so therefore, did one's dharma. Everyone was expected to do their part to make the sacrifice work; this was considered social dharma and was the beginnings of the caste system in India. The first caste was the brahmins or priests. They had the most respected job of conducting the sacrifice; therefore, they were considered the most important to society. The kshatriya caste, who were the kings and warriors, were responsible for protecting the people as well as the sacrifice. Those who produced the wealth that was required to maintain the sacrifice were called vaishya, or traders. The last and lowest caste was not directly related to the sacrifice. The shudras, or servants, were expected to serve those who maintained the sacrifice.[5] This system was believed to be God's way of maintaining order within a society. Each person was to fulfill their own duty, keeping the sacrifice and society working efficiently.

Over time, the importance of the ritual sacrifice waned and was replaced with the idea of an internal sacrifice. This was an instrumental change that enlarged the Hindu's concept of the divine, and generated the next dharmic phase in Hinduism. This is the stage were a new set of literature rose to prominence, and was even considered an extension to the original sacred Vedas. These documents collectively are called the Upanishads. Dating these scriptures, similar to the Vedas, cannot be done with any accuracy. Most scholars believe that the earliest Upanishads were written somewhere between 700-600 BC.[6] They were penned by brahmin sages who became dissatisfied with the ritual sacrifice.[7] They receded into the forest to develop their ascetic side and ponder the true meaning of life, beyond the sacrifice.

The ascetics who wrote the Upanishads used meditation techniques to reach a superconscious state of mind, a place were they personally encountered the divine within themselves. What was revealed during this process was similar to all the Hindu ascetics. They wrote about a God that didn't just set up the cosmic laws, but one who pervaded all things, holding everything and everyone together in one cosmic unity. "Truly has this universe come forth from Brahman. In Brahman it lives and has its being. Assuredly, all is Brahman." (*Chandoga* 3.14.1) But God is more than just the glue that holds everything together; he is actually more like the collective mind of all things. The *Aitareya*

Upanishad best explains this. "He is God . . . all beings, great or small, born of eggs, born from the womb, born from heat, born form soil; horses, cows, men, elephants, birds; everything that breaths, the beings that walk and the beings that walk not. The reality behind all these is Brahman, who is pure consciousness." (3.1.3) The previous religious goal of sacrificing to gain entrance into heaven was transformed into realizing that one was a part of the ultimate consciousness. According to the ascetic sages, this state is "pure unity consciousness, wherein awareness of the world and of multiplicity is completely obliterated. It is ineffable peace. It is the supreme good. It is One without a second. It is the soul. Know it alone." (*Mandukya* 1.7) The mediation and self-discipline they practiced to reach God-consciousness was deemed an internal sacrifice. These Hindus remained loyal to the Vedas; however, they reduced the previous ritual sacrifices to only a symbolic representation of the ultimate truth. The authors of the Upanishads proclaimed that the internal sacrifice was the key to salvation and supersedes the previous actual ones.

Once this transition was complete, a whole new concept of dharma emerged. Dharma was now equated with understanding the truth about God; only in this way could one live a life that reflects that truth in their actions. The *Brihadaranyaka Upanishad* proclaims, "Then he created the most excellent Law (dharma). There is nothing higher than the Law. The Law is the truth. Therefore, it is said that if a man speaks the truth he declares the Law, and if he declare the Law he speaks the truth. The Law and truth are one." (1.4.14) This dharma of the Upanishads is dependent on a new system that was previously unheard of in India. It is in the Upanishads that the development of the idea of karma, transmigration, and maya first appeared. They are key essentials to the Hindu's understanding of God. Karma is the cosmic order set up purposely by God to sustain and nurture the whole world, so that all may find their way to ultimate peace beyond death. The ascetics used the idea of accumulated merit from the ritualistic acts and took it a step further proclaiming that all actions had spiritual merits or demerits. Karma is the idea that positive merits would bring forth good things in a person's life, and negative merits, of course, just the opposite. In the real world though, it was clear that the consequences of bad or good actions did not following immediately. It was understood then, that a gap was possible between the action and the following karma consequence. From this it implicitly follows that karma could be stored up to be distributed at a later date. This idea explained the need for transmigration. If there is an excess of karmas at a person's death, then those spiritual merits or demerits carry over into the next life. In other words, the only way out of the cycle of life and death, to attain moksha, was to have a balance of zero karma. Karma and transmigration together are the system that God uses to naturally bring all people to fulfill their dharma.

The Upanishads further explain that the entire world is a forum where the soul can attach to a body so that it can live, grow, learn right from wrong, and eventually find God. The *Svetasvatara Upanishad* explains that everything from "time, space, law, chance, matter, primal energy, intelligence ... are effects, and exist to serve the soul." (1.2) If a person's soul does not learn the appropriate life lessons, then they are reborn again to have another chance to do that. Here again the world, like karma and transmigration, is considered a tool God employs to bring souls back to himself. In this way, the Hindu's look at the world as an illusion; it is what they call, maya. Just because the world is God's illusion for people to learn their lessons, does not mean we should ignore everything and everyone. Again, the *Svetasvatara Upanishad* explains this best. "Maya is thy divine consort—wedded to thee. Thou are her master, her ruler." Humans should "unitest with maya—but only for a season. Parting from her at last, thou regainest thyself." (4.5) Hindus believe that we should embrace maya as the learning tool that it is and use it to move our eternal souls closer to God. At the same time, however, they also warn us that getting too comfortable in maya only leads to despair. The real goal is not to live an easy, pampered life in maya, but to transcend maya and move closer to God-consciousness.

Enlightenment to the truth of ones connection with the divine frees a person from accumulating karma. As the *Mundaka Upanishad* says, "The deluded go round and round like the blind led by the blind."

(1.2.8) It also goes on to say, "To know him, hidden in the lotus of the heart is to untie the knot of ignorance." (2.1.10) The reasoning behind this is that bad karmas are built up from bad choices and behaviors. Basically, those who are ignorant of their true selves make poor decisions. Those who have a complete understanding of their inner selves, are able follow their true dharma and so their actions no longer accrue any karma. In this way, they are living in unison with the overall cosmic plan, helping to create harmony within the world. When this happens, then upon death that soul is finally released to salvation. People, who are ignorant of the truth, do not know how to live according to dharma, and so they are doomed to return to this life again and again. Eventually though, with the help of karma, transmigration, and maya everyone will come to realize there own true dharma and will gain moksha.

Yoga is the process of aligning oneself with dharma, and therefore gaining liberation. Yoga simply means union God. It is the path to moksha, or release beyond the cycle of rebirth. The Upanishads reveal two valid yogas that are usually used together to lead a person to liberation. The first is that of knowledge, or jnana-yoga as called by the Hindus. This is the path of mental speculation and studying. It usually requires working under a guru for many years trying to acquire spiritual knowledge. This type of yoga is just a starting point and is used in conjunction with the second type—raja-yoga. The route of raja-yoga, or mediation, leads a person to gain control over their mind and body. This is a method of searching deep within to find the connection between God and the soul. With years of practice and training, eventually knowledge and meditation will lead a person to God-consciousness.

The seers of the Upanishads had realized the final goal, but the majority of Hindu people still lived their lives according to the already defined duties and rituals that were prescribed by the brahmins. The new ideas, however, were seeping into society and soon their developed a conflict between the two. The ritualistic stance of the brahmins proclaimed duty (or dharma) to one's caste (priest, warrior, tradesman, or servant) and sacrifice as the most important things, these are worldly concerns. The mystical outlook pointed in another direction, inward. The ascetics proclaimed that true dharma could only be realized by mediation and internal sacrifice. The *Bhagavad-Gita* was composed around 250 BC when these two ways of thinking were in direct conflict with one another.[8] The *Bhagavad-Gita* is one of the most popular Hindu scriptures. This text does a superb job of blending the brahmins' ritual way of life with the newly formed mystical outlook. Most importantly though, the *Bhagavad-Gita* introduces the last phase of dharma.

The *Bhagavad-Gita* is actually a small part of the longest Hindu scripture—the *Mahabharata*. This is an epic story about a family rivalry and the ensuing war. The *Bhagavad-Gita* is revealed at the part when the warrior Arjuna is overwhelmed with a personal crisis. He stands face to face with the opposing massive army filled with his own cousins. His internal conflict is the same as the external conflict between the brahmins and the ascetics. Should Arjuna be in the world and perform his duty or should he renounce all action to live as an ascetic? It is in this tense moment that Arjuna turns to Kirshna, his charioteer, for help. Kirshna is Arjuna's spiritual guide and also an incarnation of God. It is his message to Arjuna that starts the new Hindu philosophy. This more contemporary outlook preserves the orthodox brahmin rituals and also incorporates the new mystical ideas. Even though this document supports both of the previous positions, its main function was to put forth the new one, which is the essential message of the *Gita*. In this new philosophy, called devotionalism, dharma became chiefly about devoting ones life to God. "Men who are devoted to me are in me, and I am within them." (BG 9.29) Devotionalism embraced the first two phases of dharma. Devotion to God could be shown by ritual sacrifices and the internal sacrifice. But it also went beyond these two ideas claiming that any and all of one's actions during the day, if done for God, could be considered a sacrifice to him.

Devotionalism could not have taken a hold on society without the *Bhagavad-Gita*. The God of the Upanishads was Brahman, who was described as the all-pervading reality and the underlying consciousness of everything. This is the Hindus' answer to the question "Who is

God?" but it is a difficult concept to get the mind around. It is also hard to love the impersonal. A more personal God was necessary to introduce the concepts of devotionalism. The traits of the impersonal Brahman were not lost; they were incorporated within the personal God, Kirshna, in the *Bhagavad-Gita*. Kirshna proclaimed that "I dwell deep in the heart of everyone; memory, knowledge, and reasoning come from me." (BG 15.15) He also explained to the Hindu that "I am the source of everything, and everything proceeds from me; filled with my existence, wise men realizing this are devoted to me." (BG 10.8)

With the *Bhagavad-Gita*, devotion became the most important way to God-consciousness. It became popular because it was an easier route for the ordinary person. With devotionalism, one did not have to be of the brahmin caste or renounce living an ordinary life; salvation was now made obtainable for everyone. As the *Gita* itself proclaims, "If they rely on me, Arjuna, women, commoners, men of low rank, even men born in the womb of evil reach the highest way." (BG 9.32)

The idea of devotionalism produced two new yoga paths. The first is bhakti yoga. This is a path of the heart; it is being completely in love with God. There are many ways Hindus can show their affection for God. These became the new tenants of the Hindus' faith, to be described later. Being entirely focused on God helps a person to shed their old selfish ways and move close and closer to him. Eventually, one would come to realize that there is no real separation between themselves and God. When one is bonded to God in this type of love relationship, they automatically develop an intuition for how to stay in union with the overall cosmic order and so they naturally fulfill their dharma.

The other yoga that the *Bhagavad-Gita* taught is called karma yoga, or the yoga of action. This path calls Hindus to accomplish their duties to the best of their abilities without focusing on their own personal gain. Instead, they are asked to give up the results of their actions to God. In this way then, average people, be it housewives, police officers, or merchants could fulfill their dharma by surrendering their actions to God. This system works as a type of liberation because when actions are done as a sacrifice to God, instead of feeding one's own ego, no karma accrues from them. The karma yogin evaluates each of his actions, whether they are done at home or at work, to make sure they are aligned with God's will. For Hindus who chose this path, it is a continuous struggle to be constantly aware of God's purpose. Over time, this should lead the Hindu to the discovery that it is no longer them performing actions, but God working through them.

The Vedas had laid down the elemental rudiments for the Hindu culture. The Upanishads built upon that foundation. These documents were read mostly by the upper caste. The epics and Puranas were produced to help distribute this information to the public. It was the myths, stories, gods, and heroes that were developed in these works that made popular Hinduism possible. There are two prominent epics: the *Mahabharata*, which contains the *Bhagavad-Gita*, and the *Ramayana*. These epics are stories that show how dharma is weaved into the lives of real people. Good people represent how to follow dharma; of course, then the evil characters are symbolic of adharma, which creates chaos in the world.

The Puranas came later, but much of their material could be dated to an earlier time. It was memorized and passed on orally. The bulk of this literature was written between the 4th and 6th century.$_9$ Where the epics contained heroes that were humans, the Puranas display the world of the gods. Though the Puranas have a plethora of different gods, there were really only three important ones who together form the Hindu trinity. The trinity consists of Brahma, the creator; Vishnu, the preserver; and Shiva, the destroyer. These activities—creating, preserving, and destroying—are the different functions that the all-pervading God needs to control. Hindus consider the universe to be in a constant state of flux; things are created, last a while and need to be maintained, and then reach a stage where they wither and die. This can be observed in the human life span as it goes from birth to death. It is assumed that all of Creation goes through this same routine. Keeping this continuous Creation cycle in motion, however, is considered the lower nature of God. These same processes also occur on a higher level; that is consciousness. If a person is tapped into

God, or has God-consciousness, then it is actually God that creates, maintains, and destroys one's thoughts. Within our minds, new ideas are created. We hold onto those thoughts for awhile but eventually they must die, so that we can grow and mature and have new ways of thinking. All of this happens naturally if a person has realized the goal of God-consciousness; otherwise, our thoughts are controlled by maya and lead only to a rebirth.

In the Puranas, the three main duties of God were distributed to the three gods of the trinity. Within the individual sects, however, their own god is recognized as the supreme God of the universe, handling all three functions himself. The other gods are acknowledged, but are considered more like supreme beings who are not equivalent to the godhead. The two major Hindu sects are Vaishnava and Saivism. Each of these created their own literature that became important to their followers.

The Vaishnavites see Vishnu as supreme. He is a god that is focused on law and order. They seek salvation mostly through the lens of morality and devotion. Vishnu shows his love for humans by descending to earth periodically to set things straight. There are ten popular avatars (incarnations) of Vishnu. The two most admired are Kirshna, from the *Bhagavad-Gita*, and Rama, from the *Ramayana* epic. Vishnu is described as a handsome, blue-skinned god with four arms. The blue skin gives him the image of being infinite like the sky.[10]

Vishnu assumed traits from Brahman, the god of the Upanishads, who receded into the background and was never associated specifically with any sect. Most importantly, Vishnu became the all-pervasive being, the ultimate consciousness of all reality. In their literature, the popular *Srimad Bhagavata Purana*, Kirshna (Vishnu) is described as, "Your form is pure knowledge, and your bodies are assumed for the delight of your devotees. You are the seed of everything, as well as the soul in all beings. You are everything." (10.27.11)[11] It is also declared in this same document that "those who always dedicated their desire, anger, fear, affection, sense of identity and friendship to Hari (Kirshna) enter for certain into his state of being." (10.29.15)[12]

The Saivites call God, Siva, and he is considered the ultimate reality. Siva is sometimes portrayed as sitting half-naked and cross-legged on a tiger skin with snakes wrapped around his arms. In this case, he is posed in a typical yoga stance, and the snakes too also point to his yogic power. Saivism from its beginnings has been associated with asceticism and meditation, though when devotionalism grew in popularity it also became an integral part of this sect as well. Even though Siva is visualized and represented differently from Vishnu, like Vishnu he is also seen by the Saivites to have characteristics similar to Brahman from the Upanishads. The Siva literature asks, "Where is a place that is separate from the Lord?" The answer is that no such place exists because "he is everywhere," and "his existence is not separate from the liberated soul." (*Tiruvarutpayan* of Umapati 10.15)[13] Another document states explicitly that he is "unique Consciousness which is realized as standing firm, transcending words and (ordinary) consciousness." (*Tiruvacakam* of Manikkavacakar 22.3)[14]

Both Vaishnava and Saivism use devotionalism as a means to liberation. As these sects grew in popularity, their came a need to house the different gods that were now an integral part of Hinduism. Hence, the Hindu temples sprouted up all over India to fulfill that purpose. Every aspect of the temple from the ground on up was built to denote the link between God and the soul. The ground plan generally has a sacred diagram of the cosmic man, Purusha, sitting diagonally in a large square.[15] Recall that the Creation story of Purusha was central to the ritual sacrifices. According to the myth, the universe emanated from the sacrifice of Purusha, and so the universe and Purusha are considered equivalent. God then, symbolically lies within the very foundation of the Hindu temple. Also, the sanctuary itself has its religious symbolism as it is produced to resemble a cave, and the grand, tiered roof on top of it is purposely shaped like a mountain.[16] The imagery of the cave and mountain points to the essential message of the Upanishads. The soul conceived of as small and hidden within the body is symbolically represented by a cave. In contrast to the smallness of the soul, the grandeur of the mountain signifies the universe. Within the temple, the micro-element and macro one meet together; that is, the soul and universe are united. That is the truth presented in the Upanishads. The *Chandogya Upanishad* explains this with an analogy.

"Please, sir, tell me more about the Soul."

"Be it so. Bring a fruit of that Nyagrodha tree."

"Here it is, sir."

"Break it."

"It is broken, sir."

"What do you see?"

"Some seeds, extremely small, sir."

"Break one of them."

"It is broken, sir."

"What do you see?"

"Nothing, sir."

"The subtle essence you do not see, and in that is the whole of the Nyagrodha tree. Believe me son, that that which is the sublet essence—in that have all things their existence. That is, the truth. That is the Soul. And that, Svetaketu, THAT ART THOU."(6.12.1-3)

Within the temple are located the elaborate statues of the various gods. Here is where some criticize Hindus as worshiping idols. Hindus, however, themselves do not view their statues as idols. To understand this, one must see that with devotionalism came a new understanding of God. The two new yogas that devotionalism brought to Hinduism included the idea that if a person strives to find God, to know and love God, then God will aid that person toward the goal of liberation. The *Bhagavad-Gita* tells the Hindu, "When they entrust reason to me, Arjuna, I soon arise to rescue them from the ocean of death and rebirth." (BG 12.7) Hindus who follow the devotional path believe that one way that God reaches out to his devotees is to become accessible to them through the deity statues. The statues are not whimsically created, but must be designed from the descriptions in the scriptures. There is also a ritual to call the presence of God into the statue. Hindu's then have the opportunity to show their devotion to God by bathing him, worshiping him, and leaving offerings before him. This is called *puja*. But more important than *puja*, is the idea of *darsan*. Hindus proclaim they receive *darsan* from the deity (statue). What they are getting is an actual perception of the divine. God sees his devotees through the statue's eyes and they see him.[17] There is direct contact between the human and divine within the temple walls. Other ways of showing devotion to God include: *bhajan*, devotional hymns; mantras, small repetitive prayers; and engaging in annual festivals. All of these (*darsan*, *puja*, *bhajan*, mantras and festivals) are the features of popular Hinduism today. Showing devotion to God through these techniques keeps a Hindu focused on God daily. With the aid of God, they will eventually gain God-consciousness, and will then automatically be living a life completely in sync with God.

The aim of a Hindu is coming to a realization that there is nothing in the world except God. It is the soul experiencing life lessons that are always moving it towards the ultimate goal of God-consciousness. Hindu's understand that God-consciousness is not an easy thing to obtain, nor does it happen instantaneously. The author of the *Katha Upanishad* tells them, "The ancient, effulgent being, the indwelling Spirit, subtle, deep-hidden in the lotus of the heart, is hard to know." (2.12) Just hearing about the all-pervasive God from an expert or reading about it in a book is not enough. The truth of God within must sink into the deepest corners of a person's heart, only then will a person's thinking and behavior be transformed, and only then is a person linked to the ultimate consciousness of all reality. Once this state is reached a person naturally fulfills their true dharma and obtains moksha.

BIBLIOGRAPHY

1. Basham, A. L. *The Origins and Development of Classical Hinduism.* New York: Oxford University Press, 1989. p. 21

2. Keay, John. *India a History.* New York: Grove Press, 2000. p. 25-26

3. Michaels, Axel. *Hinduism, Past and Present.* Princeton: Princeton University Press, 2004. p. 287-288

4. Knapp, Stephen. *The Power of the Dharma, An Introduction to Hinduism and Vedic Culture.* New York: iUniverse, Inc., 2006. p. 22

5. Ratnakar, Pramesh. *Hinduism.* Enberby Leiceste, LE9 5AD: Silverdale Books, 2000, p. 16

6. Basham, p. 38

7. Vesci, Uma Marina. *Heat & Sacrifice in the Vedas.* Delhi: Motilal Banarsidass Publishers, 1992, p. 286-287

8. Ratnakar, p. 23

9. Ratnakar, p. 34

10. Johnsen, Linda. *The Complete Idiot's Guide to Hinduism.* Indianapolis: Alpha Books, 2002. p. 160-161

11. Kirshna: The Beautiful Legend of God (srimad Bhagavata Purana Book X). Translated by Edwin F. Bryan. London: Penguin Books, 2003. p. 121

12. Ibid., p. 126

13. Olson, Carl ed. *Hindu Primary Sources, A Sectarian Reader.* Piscataway, NJ: Rutgers University Press, 2007. p. 477

14. Ibid., p. 457

BIBLIOGRAPHY

15. Michell, George. *The Hindu Temple, An Introduction to Its Meaning and Forms*. Chicago: The University of Chicago Press, 1988. p. 72

16. Ibid., p. 69

17. Eck, Diana L. *Darsan, Seeing the Divine Image in India*. New York; Columbia University Press, 1998. p. 6-7

CHAPTER 6:
BUDDHISM — GOD IS PEACE

Buddha was convinced that God is unknowable and unfathomable by humans; therefore, to try to define God is like groping in the dark for answers that will never be clarified. Buddha's reply to the question, "Who is God?" was that it was the wrong one. Instead, he steered his followers to pursue a different question, "How to end suffering?" According to Buddhists, once a person is born they are consigned to suffering. Today, we might call this stress. People's minds are constantly cluttered with financial worries, marital problems, or work-related issues. In order to relieve the pain of everyday life, people turn to different avenues of pleasure. Some go winnowing off to exotic vacations, while others dive deep into their work and become workaholics. Still others passionately seek happiness by accumulating more things. None of these escape routes work; they are only band-aid solutions that only ease the suffering for awhile. Eventually, the stresses of life find a way to penetrate our defenses and once again we are bombarded with a turbulent influx of worrisome thoughts. The Buddhists assert that there is a solution to our suffering. The answer is to follow Buddha's teachings, which will lead a person to ultimate peace and contentment.

Buddha never equated this peace (nirvana) with God because in his time period the word "God" was associated with too many misleading connotations, so he preferred to disregard it. If we rephrase the question to "What is the ultimate reality?" then I think it would be safe to say that for the Buddhist, this would be "the unaging, unailing, deathless, sorrowless, and undefiled supreme freedom from bondage," (*Mijjhima-Nikaya* 26:13)[1] in one word, "*nirvana*." This, then, aids in the answer to the question, "Who is God?" If we dare use the word God, then, for Buddha, it would mean an impersonal sacred reality about life, that when realized leads people to a peaceful existence.

The definition of a Buddhist is person who takes refuge in the "Triple Gem." The "Triple Gem" elements are the Buddha, the Dharma, and the Sangha.[2] These three things are the precious jewels that support a Buddhist in their journey toward nirvana. The first part of the trio, the Buddha, reminds the Buddhist that Buddha, and none other, is their spiritual guide. The name Buddha is actually a title given to the man Siddhattha Gotama. His life can probably never be reassembled in any real way today. In fact, no one knows exactly when he was born, though it is estimated it was about 560 BC.₃ Just as with other famous religious people, legends have formed about his birth and early years. But reality or not, what is available is still helpful in understanding the Buddhist faith.

Siddhattha grew up as the son of a very wealthy king. One passage in the Pali Canon refers to him as a young prince who had the luxury of living in a different palace for each season of the year. (*Anguttara-Nikaya* 1:145-146)₄ From birth, he bore thirty-two major and eighty minor marks upon his body. Because of these marks, his father's ministers predicted that he would either be a universal monarch or a spiritual savior of humankind. They claimed that if Gotama ever saw humans suffer, it would tip the scale in favor of his spiritual side. Obviously, his father wanted the boy to follow in his footsteps, so he tried to shield him from any contact with disease, old age, and death itself. Legend has it that Prince Siddhattha lived out his early years completely isolated from the world; he was not allowed outside the castle walls. The myths that surround Siddhattha's younger years also inform the Buddhist that the gods themselves plotted to find a way to bring him in contact with human suffering.₅ In reality, no one can live in their own bubble forever. Siddhattha was bound to come in contact with the uglier side of life, and probably due to his early sheltered life, it affected him more deeply then the average person. After he witnessed disease, old age, and death he made the decision to leave the comforts of the palace and go off in search of answers for these sufferings.

This was not unusual for that time period. In the sixth century BC, Northern India was experiencing a period of major social and intellectual change.[6] There were hundreds of various sects living in the Indian forests each with its own new spiritual ideas about life and salvation. (The authors of the Upanishads from the Hinduist faith were among them, but they were unique in that they remained loyal to the Vedas. All other sects claimed that sacrifice and rituals were a false way to salvation and looked to other sources.) Gotama did not immediately find enlightenment. The path to awakening was a treacherous one that almost led him to an early death. He initially joined one of the ascetic groups lead by Arada Kalama, who taught a form of mediation for "attainment of the state of nothingness." Gotama quickly mastered everything there was to know from Kalama and ascended to a position of his equal. At which point, he realized he had made a mistake and set out in search of a new group. He joined another sect and again diligently learned all there was to know about it, and once again became dissatisfied. After leaving this group, he decided to do it on his own.[7] He was determined to find the answer to suffering, so he immersed himself in the path of austerities. This meant self-mortification and fasting. He was joined by five other ascetics who believed in the same ideas.[8] He was extremely dedicated to this path, believing it would ultimately lead him to a peaceful state. After years of starving himself, however, and almost dying because of it, Gotama finally admitted defeat. He had found that indulgence in luxuries did not bring peace and neither did mortification of the body. The answer had to lie somewhere in the middle. That is why Buddha's path is called the middle way. After eating to recover his strength, Gotama was still determined to find peace. His aim, like all ascetics, was a spiritual one. He was searching for something beyond the mundane existence of everyday life. He sat under a Bodhi tree and resolved not to arise until he had attained his goal.

Gotama's movement towards enlightenment has been described as the three stages of cognition. The first cognition was the ability to see all of his past lives. Gotama visualized himself belonging to different clans, having different names, and different appearances. Next, he acquired the second cognition—psychic vision—which enabled him to perceive the birth and rebirth of humans everywhere. With this came the understanding that good karma leads to a happy rebirth and evil karma causes a miserable one. Lastly, and most importantly, Gotama acquired the third cognition, which was the ability to exterminate the things that tainted his life. With this realization, he was released from suffering and obtained nirvana. According to legend, after Buddha attained enlightenment, the earth moved, the thunder boomed, rain fell from a clear sky, and the heavens showered him with blossoms.[9]

Once awakened to the reality of life, he was called Buddha. From then on, he emanated peace and was in a position to educate the world about how to end suffering.

This first gem of Buddhism, Buddha, is commemorated on a festival called Wesak Day, or in the West, Buddha Day. On the day of the full moon in May, Buddhists celebrate the birth, enlightenment, and death of Buddha. This holiday is a joyful one. Temples are usually decorated with lanterns, and Buddha statues are adorned with flowers. Some Buddhists bring offerings of flowers or candles and lay them at the foot of the Buddha statue. Another ritual that pertains to this holiday is to pour water or tea over the infant Buddha statue, representing the rain that fell and bathed the newborn baby, Buddha, the day he was born. In monasteries, Buddha's life is remembered through talks, sermons, or plays performed so that the children can learn all about him. The entire theme of the day is to give reverence to Buddha and his life.

The second important Buddhists' gem is the Dharma; that is the teachings of Buddha. At first, Buddha wavered about teaching. During his enlightenment process, he had a clear picture of the complete delusion that encompassed the world. The task of overcoming all of that seemed overwhelming at first, but out of compassion for the world Buddha decided he would take it to task.

Buddha and his monks were initially just another ascetic group like so many other sects of the time. In contrast to the other groups that kept their teachings as secret as possible, however, Buddha sent his monks out into the world with the mission of bringing as many people as possible to enlightenment. This was not done out of pride, but compassion for the suffering. It was obvious that Buddha genuinely cared about people regardless of race, caste, or gender and he spoke directly to them in terms they could understand. It was his teaching ability, knowledge, compassion, and certainty of his path that helped spread Buddhism.[10] Even after his death his teachings remained on.

According to Buddhist tradition, a first council convened soon after Buddha's death in order to preserve his teachings. It was held at Rajagaha, a village in modern state of Bihar, and attended by five hundred Arahats (enlightened ones). The leader of the council first questioned the monk Upali on the Vinaya, a code of discipline for the monks, and then in a like manner asked the monk Anada to recite the Dharma, that is Buddha's teachings. This oral information was remembered and held in high esteem as the official words of Buddha.[11] Unfortunately, nothing tangible remains from this council since society at the time was still orally based. The Pali Canon, though, is the one of the earliest Buddhist canons that is still utilized today. The Theravada Buddhists treasure this document, for them, it contains all the original wisdom of Buddha. The Pali Canon includes the two sections articulated at the first Buddhist council, the Vinaya and the

Sutta (or Dharma). In addition, it also has a third collection added later called the Abhidharma, which further clarifies Buddha's teachings.

In the Pali Canon, Buddha's first sermon to his five ascetic friends is preserved. This sermon is so important to the Theravada tradition that they have a special day called Asala Day to remember it. The western Buddhists call this festival, Dharma Day. In his first discourse, Buddha laid out the essential teachings of the four noble truths. These are the truths that if fully understood, have the capability to lead followers to ultimate peace. Everything Buddha taught resonated from these four truths. They are:

1. The noble truth of suffering
2. The noble truth of the origin of suffering
3. The noble truth of the cessation of suffering.
4. The noble truth of the path that leads to the cessation of suffering.

These statements may appear overly simplified at first, but each one holds a wealth of information.

The first noble truth explains simply that to live is to suffer. This may seem pessimistic, but hiding our suffering in the deepest corners of our mind does nothing to solve the problem. The first step to ending suffering must be to accept that it happens. In today's society, similar to how Gotama grew up, the realities of old age, sickness, and death are ignored. Aging is something that no one wants to accept as a fact of life, so they buy creams to eliminate wrinkles, dyes to change hair color, and even plastic surgery to appear more youthful. Sick people are placed in hospitals under the care of professionals, and all but forgotten except by loved ones. Death itself is a topic which no one discusses. Unlike some societies where it is typical to have a mourning period of wearing black, in our society we can put on our black attire in the morning, attend a funeral, and are back in a business suit by lunch. The dead are quickly buried and forgotten. There is a pervasive philosophy that it is better to get on with living than to focus on death. Buddha's point was just the opposite. His first noble truth purposely opened up the forbidden door that suffering was hiding behind and let out all the monsters therein. Truly people are afraid of getting sick, growing old, and the ultimate fear, of course, is death. Buddha described suffering in detail so that people would be motivated to change.

According to Buddha there are three types of suffering. The first is suffering to suffer and is easily understood. Someone pinches you and you feel the pain.[12] That is suffering. But the important thing that Buddha brought to light is that there is a difference between physical pain and suffering. We will never be released from all physical pains because there will always be accidents, sicknesses, or people who want to harm us. Suffering though is different than pain; it is done in the mind when it thinks, "I want this to stop." It is the dislike of pain that causes us to suffer.

The second type of suffering is suffering of change.[13] We naturally want things to remain as they are, especially if life is good to us. If we have a good relationship, well-behaved children, and lots of material possessions we get fooled into thinking that life is great. The problem comes when the relationship fails, the children misbehave, and the material things deteriorate, get stolen, or are broken. The point is that nothing ever stays the same; life is constantly changing. The Buddhists have a word for this; they say every thing is impermanent. If we like things to stay the same, then we are going to suffer when they change.

The last type is called pervasive suffering. This third level is more difficult to identify as it does not feel like suffering. It is due to ignorance of the truth. This suffering happens because people are born with five aggregates. These aggregates are the body and the four mental states of feelings, perception, mind, and consciousness.[14] The problem is that most people believe these aggregates to collectively be an "I." What Buddha did was to look at each one separately and realize that this is not "I," this is not "I," and this is not "I." Therefore, an "I" does not really exist. It is our constant need to grasp at a self, in order to protect our self image, which causes us to suffer. Buddha taught that there was no self.

After having a complete understanding of suffering, then the second noble truth is an investigation into what causes suffering. Buddha explains that it is our cravings that cause suffering. There are three types of cravings that all need to be abandoned if suffering is to stop. The first is the desire to collect things or to feel pleasure. Basically, in one word it is greed.[15] This is the attachment to delicious food, expensive cars, having sex, beautiful homes, or nice clothes. Most of the time people go through life looking for the next thing to attach their minds too. If someone has an expensive car, then he wants the beautiful woman. If a person has married the supermodel, next he wants the huge house to go with it. After procuring all those things, he still yearns for a better car or to redecorate his house. Eventually, one has to get off the cycle of grasping for something more.

The next type of craving is called craving for existence. This is the thirst for the "I" that is not really there. It is the ego that wants to present itself to the world in a certain way.[16] For example, I am smart, I am good at sports, or I am a doctor. The snag comes when these things fail us. When we get fired from the doctor's position, when we fail a test, or lose a game then we suffer because we thought those things determined who we were. When actually there is no "I" that needs to be defined. In this case, it is our ignorance of reality that causes us to suffer.

The last type of craving is just the opposite, it is craving for annihilation. This is the wish for something bad to stop.[17] If you don't want your parents divorced, or you don't want to go to school, then you suffer. This type of craving can lead to frustration and anger over things that one has no power to control.

The key to enlightenment is the eradication of the cravings, and understanding that these desires arise because of ignorance of the ultimate reality of life. The third noble truth states that there is a solution to this ignorance and when applied, it will lead to enlightenment. The lasting peace gained by enlightenment is called nirvana. People often misunderstand nirvana as the annihilation of the person, since Buddha described it as "blowing out." What this really means is the cessation of suffering. Nirvana is not a reward or a place; it is a state of mind. Nirvana is something that will emerge only through the development of wisdom. This concept of nirvana is very difficult to understand and Buddha did not spend a lot of time explaining the exact details of it. That is because he believed it could not be fully understood until it was realized. But he did say that it was "unaging, unailing, deathless, sorrowless and undefiled supreme freedom from bondage." (*Mijjhima-Nikaya* 26:13)[18] According to Buddhists, the second cognitive phase of Buddha's enlightenment proved that rebirth was the fate of anyone who did not attain nirvana. Buddha's path was the way off the cycle of reincarnation and a direct route to everlasting peace.

The fourth and last noble truth is the summit that the other truths have been converging in on. It is the heart of Buddha's teaching; it is the path to enlightenment. This noble truth declares that the eight-fold path, if followed correctly, leads to the cessation of suffering. It is called the eight-fold path because, obviously, it has eight parts; they are right speech, right action, right livelihood, right effort, right mindfulness, right concentration, right view, and right thought. These eight parts of the path are normally broken down into three trainings which include ethics, meditation, and wisdom.

Buddhism does not define a specific set of morality laws to follow; instead, the Buddhist philosophy is to always be aware of the feelings, perspective, and rights of other people.[19] When this approach to life is adopted, it results in positive karma. Accruing good karma is the first step toward the path of peace. The guidelines for this are the three components of the ethics training that is right speech, right action, and right livelihood. Right speech means contemplating your words carefully. It could simply be the precepts of do not lie and do not gossip. But really it means much more than that; it is consciously choosing to use gentle, kind words when speaking to others. Right action pertains to the things we do with our body. Again, it could be basically the rules do not cheat, do not commit adultery, and do not steal, but on a higher level it means using our actions to show compassion for people. Right livelihood has to do with the kind of job one takes. For example, in Buddhism they don't believe in hurting animals and so to become a butcher would produce bad karma.

After ethics, the next part of the training is on mediation. Buddha said,

> I do not perceive even one thing, O monks, that is so unwieldy as the undeveloped mind. An undeveloped mind is truly unwieldy.
>
> I do not perceive even one thing, O monks, that is so wieldy as the developed mind. A developed mind is truly wieldy.
>
> I do not perceive even one thing, O monks, that leads to such great harm as an undeveloped mind. An undeveloped mind leads to great harm.
>
> I do not perceive even one thing, O monks, that leads to such great benefit as a developed mind. A developed mind leads to great benefit. (Anguttara-Nikaya1.1-4)[20]

Mastering the mind through meditation is of crucial importance because it brings the required stillness and undistracted focus needed to gain wisdom, which leads to ultimate peace. Mediation training includes the next three parts of the path including right effort, right mindfulness, and right concentration. Right effort is having the energy, enthusiasm, and belief in the noble eight-fold path. Buddha knew that he could not liberate anyone. What he had gained was the tools to reach enlightenment, but only a person applying the tools to the job could be successful. In this respect, right effort really applies to all three trainings, but within meditation it is important to have the determination to continue even when it gets difficult. Right mindfulness and right concentration are used together as a team during meditation. Concentration is the willed intention to force the mind to focus on a single object. It is actually the servant behind the real master which is mindfulness. Mindfulness is the ability to look critically at ones thoughts and actions in the present moment. It is mindfulness that can pinpoint one's selfishness, one's suffering, and one's internal defensive lies. Mindfulness, if practiced diligently, can break through our protective coverings and into the inner reality where wisdom can be found. It is concentration, though, that allows mindfulness to do its work. Without concentration, our mind would wander sporadically from idea to idea, or be consumed with worries which can block mindfulness from being productive.

The final training is what everything thus far on the eight-fold path has been leading up too, and that is wisdom. To gain wisdom, one must understand that to end suffering their must be an annihilation of cravings, which cause defiled thoughts such as greed, hatred, and selfishness. This can only be accomplished by overcoming our ignorance, which penetrates deep into a person's psyche. Buddha taught that our unwholesome states have three layers. They are the stage of latent tendency, the stage of manifestation, and the stage of transgression. The first training in moral discipline cuts out the stage of transgression. That is, Buddhists who have mastered this level are no longer speaking or acting on their cravings since they have obtained the right speech, right actions, and right livelihood. The second training of meditation is supposed to wipe out the stage of manifestation. That is, these Buddhists would no longer have any conscious-defiled thoughts since they have the right effort, right mindfulness, and right concentration. The problem is, however, that there still might be some subconscious defilement. It is the training in wisdom that finally gives Buddhists the capability to eliminate even the latent tendencies. The reason is that ignorance has a very powerful hold on people and it is the driving factor causing dangerous feelings, the worst of which are greed and anger. Ignorance can only be completely eliminated by wisdom.[21] To gain wisdom Buddhists must have the right view of life; that is, the understanding of the true nature of reality as impermanent and ever changing. Buddha recognized that our entire reality is bound up completely in our thoughts. Having the right view leads to the right thoughts; this is wisdom.

Ignorance has a strong grip on people. This is because people crave the safety of something permanent and lasting. The impermanence of reality seems terrifying at first, especially when applied at the personal level. The no-self concept, though, is the very heart of Buddha's teachings. In society, we call ourselves "I" so that we know who we are talking about, but the Buddhists proclaim that in reality there is no permanent "I." Buddha taught that from moment to moment a person is constantly changing, meaning there is never a fixed, solid person. Remember back to when you were a child. You were small and had immature thoughts, but every day you grew a little and matured a little. Now as an adult, you are not the same person you were as a child. Your body is different, your thoughts and actions are different, and *you* are completely different. According to Buddhists, it is the same for adults; they continue to change, only on a much smaller scale. In fact, science has shown that in seven years, all our old cells have died and we have a whole different physical body with all new cells. There is absolutely no solid "I" at any moment in time.

The idea that the self is constantly changing means that it is empty of any real solid substance, but that does not imply that people do not exist. The Buddhists believe that nothing is independent, standing all by itself. This is the emptiness of everything. All people and things are empty by themselves, but if one looks at the bigger picture, there is a fullness to the world where everything is alive due to its interdependence on each other. For example, a flower could not bloom unless there is a seed, but it also takes soil, water, and sunshine. Without those things, there would be not flowers. Once a person fully grasps this and acts on that understanding, then they have gained wisdom. With wisdom comes nirvana, supreme peace now and for eternity.

The earliest Buddhists, the Theravada tradition, valued Buddha as the wisest human to walk the earth. They believed that through his enlightenment, he gained wisdom and nirvana. Since Buddha left the world, the only thing his disciples could grab onto for support was his teachings. The Theravada Buddhists exempted Buddha's teaching from impermanence, and made them the only real, true essence in the world. This information was preserved in the Pali Canon so that people could use it to guide them to nirvana.

For many, however, the idea that dharma, the teachings of Buddha, was the ultimate, essence of life seemed to impersonal. Instead, these people claimed that even Buddha's teachings were also empty of all essence. They turned to something more personal, the Buddha himself. They saw Buddha's compassion, instead of wisdom, as his most important characteristic. This group of people eventually became known as the Mahayana sect. They perceived Buddha not just as a human role model, but as a man that had touched people's hearts so deeply that there appeared to be something superhuman about him. The Mahayana sect was unable to accept Buddha's death, and believe that he is still a mystical part of the world continuing to guide all people toward enlightenment.

> The Buddha's body fills the cosmos, Appearing before all beings everywhere—In all conditions, wherever sensed, reaching everywhere, Yet always on this seat of enlightenment. (*Avatamsaka Sutra*)[22]

This idea developed into the concept of buddha-nature, which brought hope to the average person that they could obtain the goal of peace. The Mahayanist Buddhists believe that even though there is suffering, everyone still has an innate Buddha-nature that can be realized. This is a natural inclination to be able to obtain enlightenment. All one has to do is remove ignorance, greed, and anger. For what is peace except the elimination of these bad emotions, which seem to have a dominating grip over people's lives. Once these corrupt mental states are gone, then there is nothing left, except love. In other words, nothing needs to be added; a person is born with everything they need to obtain peace. This understanding of buddha-nature helps Buddhists to see the equality of all people. An awareness that others are not so different from oneself makes it easier to replace hatred with compassion, brining peace not only to oneself, but to others as well.

Compassion, rather than searching for wisdom, became the central focus of the Mahayana sect. This changed their main objective from gaining enlightenment, to working toward removing suffering from all people. Those who reached enlightenment, but did not disappear into eternal nirvana, were given the title Bodhisattva. They purposely remained in the world to continue to help others obtain ultimate peace. This is such a huge task that it may never be fully accomplished. Out of devotion for the world, though, a Bodhisattva makes this his mission. Over time, many different spiritual heroes, or Bodhisattvas, became popular within this sect, and were available for the average person to call on for help. According to the Mahayana sect, the compassion of the Bodhisattva should be the highest spiritual aspiration. In this way, the self was de-emphasized and a worldly commitment to all humans obtaining enlightenment became the ultimate goal.

Buddha was both a wise and compassionate man. With him as an example, it is obvious that one would need both of those characteristics in order to obtain peace. Looking at the eight-fold path that Buddha taught confirms that this is true. The initial training in ethics focuses on compassion and the final parts of the path, right view and right thoughts, teach wisdom. Wisdom and compassion, however, are not really two separate entities; they are intimately connected. Developing wisdom helps build compassion. It is our self-centeredness—the distinctive "I"—that is not really there, that leads one away from compassion and toward selfish thoughts. Once this delusion of a solid self is removed, it opens up one's heart to compassion.[23]

Returning again to the Buddhists' "Triple Gem," the last treasure that supports a Buddhist's faith is the Sangha; this is the Monastery

Buddhist communities. From its beginnings, Buddhism was based in the monastery, where Buddha taught his instructions to those who left their homes to dedicate their lives to the teachings. In Thailand, the Buddhists commemorate the importance of the Sangha on a festival called Magha Puja Day; in the west this holiday is associated with Sanha Day. This day is significant because it recalls when 1,250 disciples of Buddha gathered together, without being called. All those present were enlightened people who were ordained by Buddha personally. Marking this day as even more special was the fact that it occurred when the moon was full. For this reason, Magha Puja is still celebrated during a full moon. Magha Puja recalls that Buddha delivered an important sermon to these monks, giving them the rules and regulations of the monastic order. The monasteries were originally founded by Buddha himself and still have an important part in Buddhism. The monks and nuns are role-models for how to live the dharma. Lay people naturally respect them as a pillar of strength, for the ordained are their spiritual guides helping people move closer to their goal of peace.

A Buddhist has faith that, by taking refuge in the "Triple Gem," and especially in Buddha and his teachings on the four noble truths, they can achieve eternal peace. Basically, this requires the elimination of the corrupt thoughts of greed, anger, and ignorance that cover their inner buddha-nature. The result of eliminating these pollutants is a content life, no matter whether rich or poor, sick or healthy. They will have an unending calm attitude regardless of the turbulence that might spring up around them. In addition, they will have gained wisdom of the reality of the emptiness of all things, or in other words, the interdependence of everything. This enlightenment leads to the activity of compassion; that is working toward not just their own peace but also ending suffering for all humanity.

BIBLIOGRAPHY

1. Bodhi, Bhikkhu. *In the Buddha's Words, an Anthology of Discourses from the Pali Canon*. Boston: Wisdom Publications, 2005. p. 56

2. Yun, Hsing. *Lotus in a Stream*. Tokyo: Weatherhill, 2000. p. 65

3. Reat, Noble Ross. *Buddhism A History*. Berkeley: Asian Humanities Press, 1951. p. 6

4. Ibid., p 7

5. Ibid., p. 8

6. Robinson, Richard H. *The Buddhist Religion, a Historical Introduction*. Belmont: Wadsworth Publishing Company, 1997. p. 7

7. Bodhi, 56-58

8. Reat, p. 10

9. Robinson, p. 15-17

10. Ibid., p. 43-44

11. Ibid., p. 51-52

12. Tsering, Geshe Tashi. *The Four Noble Truths, The Foundation of Buddhist Thought*. Boston: Wisdom Publications, 2005. p. 34

13. Ibid., p. 34-35

14. Ibid., p. 36-37

15. Harvey, Peter. *An Introduction to Buddhism, Teachings, History and Practices*. Cambridge: Cambridge University Press, 1990, p. 53

16. Ibid., p. 53

BIBLIOGRAPHY

17. Ibid., p. 53

18. Bodhi, p.56

19. Tsering, p. 126

20. Bodhi, 267

21. Bodhi, Bhikkhu. *The Noble Eight-fold Path the Way to the End of Suffering.* Kandy, SRI Lanka: Buddhist Publication Society, 1998. p. 26

22. Clearly, Thomas, *The Flower Ornament Scripture: A Translation of the Avatmasaka Sutra.* Boston: Shambhala, 1993. p. 162

23. Gyatso, Tenzin. *The Compassionate Life.* Boston: Wisdom Publications, 2001. p. 23

CHAPTER 7:
TAOISM—GOD IS THE ENERGY OF LIFE

Much of our lives are normally governed by what is typically called "the rat race." That is a constant battle to get ahead, to make money, and to become successful. At what expense do we run this race? We risk possible heart attacks, strokes, high blood pressure, and depression. We can get in the habit of going through life as if on autopilot, all the while draining our energy that could be used for something better. We do what the world expects us to by chasing after empty goals, which ultimately wastes our energy and leads us toward death instead of life. One of Taoism's first scriptures has a good explanation of this situation.

"By indulging in what is frivolous and superficial, they bring desolation and harm upon themselves and can't finish the years heaven has designed for them. The many activities latter-born men are involved in are needless and risky. So men are always in a rush, unable to come to a halt. . . . Much embellishment has brought forth corruption and fraud. Furthermore, men cause distress by trying to outdo each other, and they let corruption and jealousy arise in their midst. Within, they have lost their true state." (*Taiping Ching 44.42*)[1]

This religion is first and foremost about nourishing life. More than any other religion they are focused on this life and living it to its fullest and longest. The Taoists see God as the very energy that is found in all living things. They, however, do not use the word God; instead, they call this energy source the Tao. It can be seen in the constant movement throughout the universe. The Tao is what causes the planets to circulate around the sun, and it moves the water through its natural cycle. The Tao also changes the weather from one season to the next, and alternates the day and night. When humans are in harmony with the natural order of things, they can experience a life that is spontaneous and free from pressures, worries, and demands. By living this way, a person has a meaningful, long life. Upon death, they then go on to an eternity in union with the Tao.

The Taoist religion formed in China during turbulent times when the Han Dynasty was crumbling under the strain of corrupt, weak rulers. At the same time, flood and drought were killing the peasant's crops, causing hunger and serfdom to prevail. Desperate times called for desperate behavior and peasant uprisings were a norm during this period. This was the stage that was set when a new scripture called

Taiping qing ling shu (The Book of Great Peace) entered the picture. The book was written from the point of view of a "Celestial Master" who was educating one of his disciples with a heavenly plan, that if instituted would bring forth a period of great peace. It was presented to Emperor Shun (ruled 125 to 144 AD) by Gong Chong who represented his teacher Gan Ji, who was known as a fang-shi or an expert in the supernatural.[2] Unfortunately, the messenger died a lonely death in prison without the knowledge that eventually, his master's book would become the basis for a new movement that would change the face of Chinese religion forever.

It was a man named Chang Tao-ling who tried to implement the ideas proposed in that text. He was motivated in this task because in 142 AD, he had received a revelation from God, Lord Lao, who appointed him the title "Celestial Master," and established a covenant with him on the basis of working toward great peace. As the scripture emphasized, the new religion was based on heralding a time of great peace, instigated by the good morals and spiritual health of all the members in society. In this venue, Chang Tao-ling called for people to take responsibility for their own actions through confession of sins and certain penance rituals. He also proposed that if people developed their inner and outer spirituality, they would be free from illness and live a long life.

Chang Tao-ling presented himself to his group as a healer. His healing capabilities were based on using talisman holy water which connected him to the shamans of that period. Furthermore, he was born and studied in Southern China, which is well known for its shamanism.[3] Clearly, there was a shamanistic influence in Chang Tao-ling's sect. Shamanism and Taoism have some similarities. Both see the world as full of cosmic forces and both want to live their lives connected with them. Taoism, however, sees a connection between the different forces, something like an ultimate driver of all of them. That is the Tao. In an early document from this sect, called the Celestial Masters, the Tao is described as follows:

> The great Tao is that which encompasses heaven and earth, is joined with and nourishes all forms of life, and controls the myriad initiatory mechanisms. Without shape or image it is undifferentiated and yet spontaneously gives birth to the million species. Though it is something to which humans cannot put a name, from heaven and earth on down everything is born and dies through the Tao. (*Commands and Admonitions for the Families of the Great Dao* HY 788 12a)[4]

The Celestial Masters understood the Tao to be the transcendent power behind all of Creation, the one who gives order and direction to all of life. The Tao is what gives Taoism its name, and is at the very foundation of the religion. This idea of the Tao, though, did not originate with Chang and his group. Even before him, Taoism had been a philosophy that had already made an impact on the Chinese government. Chang Tao-ling's new religion was based not only on the *Taiping Ching,* but also on the Taoist philosophy, especially as it laid out in the *Tao Te Ching.* This document is the most famous of Taoist scriptures and its origins are still shrouded in mystery.

To try and get as clear picture as we can of this document, as well as the entire Taoist philosophy, we need to backtrack to a time in China's history called the warring states (475–221 BC). This was, again, a period of great strife and uncertainty. The political upheaval and fast social changes forced the human intellect to its furthest capacities and all sorts of new ideas and philosophies emerged in China. All focused on the same question, "What is the way?" "The way" refers to the way that government should be organized and the way that people are expected to behave.[5] A number of schools of thought arose in response to that question; so many in fact, that the Chinese call them collectively the "hundred schools."[6] Taoism arose in this situation as a response to a world that seemed crazy and out of control; their initial reaction was to escape to nature and become hermits. The trees, mountains, and rivers comforted them and cleared their minds of all anxiety. It may have been in this peaceful setting that they were able to sort out their own meaning of life.[7]

Among these people, Yang Chu's name stands out as possibly the first Taoist; though, this is a title given to him in retrospect. When exactly he lived his life may be impossible to get a true date, but by reference from other philosophers we can estimate that he must have lived sometime between 470 and 300 BC. Yang Chu represents the earliest Taoist philosophy, but he did not leave behind any definite works that were attributed to him. From other philosophers of the time, however, we can gather some information on what he believed. Han-fei-ta, from the third century, commented on Yang Chu and his philosophy, saying, "There is a man whose policy it is not to enter a city which is in danger, nor to remain in the army. Even for the great profit of the whole world, he would not exchange one hair of his shank . . . He is one who despises things and values life." We also have the words of a second-century philosopher Huai-nan-tzu who gives us, "Preserving life and maintaining what is genuine in it, not allowing things to entangle ones person: this is what Yang Chu established."[8] It appears that Yang Chu found comfort in the simple things of life, seeing power and riches as being a danger to one's health. According to him, a person's most important treasure was their life which was to be safeguarded at all costs. These ideas are the very beginnings on which Taoism was built; for above all else a Taoist sees the Tao as life.

When someone nurtures their life properly, then they naturally fall in sync with the Tao. These ideas became integrated into the eternal truth of Taoism as it moved from its initial phase of escape to living in harmony within society.

The second phase of reintegrating back into society is best characterized by the Taoist philosophy of the *Tao Te Ching*. Who exactly wrote it and when was it written are still being debated. An estimation for the dating of the document would fall somewhere in the range from the late fourth century BC to early third century BC.[9] Legend says that it was written by Lao Tzu, which simply means "aged one." Most recent data, however, tends to suggest that there probably was no man by the name Lao Tzu, but that this name was applied to the work because it represented the wisdom passed down from age to age from the ancient ones.[10]

This document, then, is possibly a conglomeration of ideas coming from the different schools of the time with an emphasis on Yang Chu's views of simplicity and longevity, as well as some ancient Chinese religious ideas. All of these thoughts were unified together around a common theme of the Tao. This is the first Taoist document that explores the meaning and function of the Tao. In doing this, it not only answers the question of how to live a safe, long life, but also sets up some of the important cosmology that is foundational to the Taoist religion.

The Chinese, from early on, had already segregated the world into three parts consisting of heaven, earth, and humanity. The *Tao Te Ching* organized these three ideas around the Tao, with the Tao given the highest priority. It says:

> Humans follow the earth,
> The Earth follows heaven,
> Heaven follows the Tao,
> Tao follows self-becoming. (25.4)

A vivid picture of the eternal truth of Taoism begins with and understanding of the Tao. First, it should be made clear that for the Taoist, the Tao cannot be described through language because that is how humans describe things of this world. There are no words that can fully characterize the Tao. In the very first section of *Tao Te Ching*, the author tries to explain this:

> Tao that can be spoken of,
> Is not the everlasting Tao.
> Name that can be named,
> Is not the Everlasting name. (1.1)

The Tao is beyond human wisdom, beyond description, and beyond language. At the same time, the Taoist continues to try to describe the indescribable. It is not something you can see and grab a hold of; it is formless and subtle. Originally the Tao was one primordial chaos that eventually divided into two energies, the yin and yang.

> One gives birth to two,
> Two gives birth to three
> Three gives birth to ten thousand beings.
> Ten thousand beings carry yin on their backs and embrace yang in their front, blending these two vital breaths to attain harmony.(42.1)

The yin/yang philosophy is probably as ancient as China. Yang is associated with heaven, strength, and activity, and the yin is closer to the earth, passivity, and weakness. Combining and mixing yin and yang energies then gives rise to the thousands of things that are created such as humans, plants, animals, and all the things of the natural world.

This characterization of the Tao as a pair of energies gets to the very heart of Taoism. The world was not created to be chaotic and out of control. It is through these two energies working together in harmony that the world is kept functioning properly. The Taoist believes that there are no pure yin or yang energies in the world; everything is a blending of both. In nature, we see this process in action with the constant movement from day to night. We can get a glimpse that they are united by the transition point of twilight where there is a combination of both day and night. Normally, we think of day and night as two separate entities. For the Taoist, though, they believe that one actually includes the other. If we consider yin to be night and yang to be day, then as yin increases it gets darker and darker but there is always a portion of yang energy still present. Eventually, yin will reach its max at midnight, then it will decrease and yang will increase.

The cyclical pattern of the expansion and contraction of the yin and yang energies is the very breath of the Tao itself. In order to live a fulfilled, long life a Taoist must tap into the natural rhythms of the Tao; for to do otherwise produces chaos. That then leads to stress, illness, and a shortened life span. Not because there is some god sitting in heaven punishing us for not behaving according to his laws, but because that is the way that the world was fashioned to be. One example of how most people naturally live in union with the Tao can be seen within the simple routine of sleeping at night and being active during the day. With the light of day, people are naturally more awake, but as the day wanes they become tired and sleep during the night. This all happens with out one having to think about it. People don't usually spend time calculating when their bodies should rest. If, however, one becomes an adversary to the natural pattern of the Tao by working nightshifts and sleeping during day, then their bodies would begin to function improperly. These workers might suffer from insomnia or excessive sleepiness resulting in crankiness; this may damage their marriage and other social relationships. There is also the health risk of gastrointestinal disorders.[11] All of this occurs because they were not in harmony with the Tao. For the Taoists, remember, eternal truth focuses on the Tao as life, and therefore being connected with it results in a healthy, long life.

Wu-wei is a term used to denote the vital principal that Taoist use to live a life in the flow of the Tao. *Wu-wei* is usually translated as non-action. This is because when a Taoist is one with the Tao, they appear to be doing very little action in order to achieve their goals. It's not because they don't have goals or they are lazy, but in fact the Taoist concept of *wu-wei* is a way of working smart and expending as little energy as possible. The idea is to see problems before they arise and fix them when they are small and manageable. This is explained in the *Tao Te Ching* as, "plan the difficult while it is easy. Accomplish the great when it is small." (63.2)

An example might help to clarify: Think of a teenage who has never been properly disciplined from a young age. He will probably be unruly and difficult to handle. If, however, the parents were smart, they would teach their child from a very young age to treat them and their rules with respect. When this is the case, it seems like the parents effortlessly know how to rear their child to adulthood. Another important thing to remember in this is to be aware of change before it happens, thus to be sensitive to the slightest movement in things. Again, using the image of parenting, a parent must notice when a child is transitioning from one phase to another. Parents who use the *wu-wei* philosophy would realize that their child is growing and maturing and treat them differently ever step of the way, for dealing with a teenager as if they were a small child would only lead to disaster.

Wu-wei contains the fundamental paradox of Taoism. In performing very little action, everything seems to get done. The *Tao Te Ching* explains it this way:

> To pursue learning one increased daily
> To pursue Tao one decreased daily
> To decrease and again to decrease
> Until one arrives at not doing (*wu-wei*)
> Not doing (*wu-wei*) and yet nothing is not done. (48.1)

The idea of decreasing is to be losing our selfish ways. When we surrender our selves more and more, we can gain more and more of the natural ways of the Tao. This should include giving up the desire to be rich, famous, and powerful. For people who cling to those things are furthest from the Tao.

> Wearing embroidered clothes,
> Carrying sharp swords,
> Being surfeited with foods and drinks.
> To accumulate wealth and treasures in excess,
> This is called robbery and crime.
> This is not to follow the Tao. (53.2)

Being greedy has many problems to it. First, by hoarding things to themselves, a person upsets the natural balance of how the Tao distributes the appropriate goods to everyone. Second, the more stuff one collects the more time and energy they have to put into maintaining their things. The biggest problem with being greedy, though, is that it has a never-ending effect of keeping the mind focused on gratifying one's wants. The *Tao Te Ching* makes clear how important it is to be content.

> Among offenses, non is greater than having what is desirable.
> Among calamites, non is greater than not knowing contentment.
> Among blames, non is greater than the desire for gain.
> Therefore the contentment that comes from knowing contentment is long lasting contentment. (46.2)

A person practicing *wu-wei* would naturally see that greed ostracizes one from the Tao; on the other hand, they would also realize that being content would bring them closer to the Tao.

Being noncontending is another aspect of *wu-wei* that steers one in the right direction toward the Tao. According to the *Tao Te Ching*, a person should strive to do good, but never succumb to using the wrong means to attain the goal.

> The good person is resolute only,
> But dares not take the path of the strong
> Be resolute yet do not boast
> Be resolute yet do not show off
> Be resolute yet do not be haughty,
> Be resolute because you have no choice,
> Be resolute yet do not overpower. (30.3)

A Taoist realizes that eventually the "soft and weak overcome the hard and strong" (36.2), but they must have patience in the meantime. A person who has implemented *wu-wei* in their life draws near to the Tao because they are selfless, peaceful, humble, and live a modest life. *Wu-wei*, then, is how the Taoist implements their eternal truth of living in harmony with the subtle forces of the Tao, which automatically result in health, happiness, peace, and everlasting life.

An important way for a Taoist to promote *wu-wei* in their daily lives is through stillness. This quietude is again a natural response to the movement of the Tao. With time, our lives generally grow more and more confused or out of sync with the Tao. When this point reaches its natural expansion, it is time to reverse the chaos and move toward quietude, which has the effect of clarifying things and bringing them back in tune with the Tao. Without this constant spiritual renewal, a person can become drained and overwhelmed by the pressures of life. Again, we see the negative effect on the body when a person is not in the flow of the Tao. The opposite is also believed to be true too; that is, a person can maintain their health by being aligned with the Tao. A Taoist, then, should make a habit of making time for stillness in their life. This time of quietude is so important that it is associated with recovering life, and gaining the everlasting. The *Tao Te Ching* says:

> Each again returns to its root
> To return to the root is to attain quietude
> It is called to recover life.
> To recover life is to attain the Everlasting
> To know the everlasting is to be illumed. (16.2)

The function of stillness is to clear a person's mind of their problems and stress, so that it can become receptive to the voice of the Tao. In this way, a Taoist relies not so much on their own intellect, but more on their intuition which is linked to the Tao.

The *Tao Te Ching* is divided into two sections. The first, as described above, explains about the Tao and its natural cycles. The second part emphasizes the concept of *te*. Notice that the two important ideas that the *Tao Te Ching* illuminates are both a part of its title—that is the "Tao" and the "*te*." *Te* has been translated either as "power" of the Tao, or "virtue" of the Tao, and it emanates from the Tao. It is the inherent potential given to all at birth, which helps people function in alignment with the Tao. For this reason, it is to be treasured and developed. If not nurtured, then *te* decreases diminishing one's connection to the Tao. Basically, *te* is the power that helps people maintain *wu-we*. This is summed up by the phrase, "the power (te) of non-contention (wu-wei)." (68.2) That, in a nutshell, is the main idea of the *Tao Te Ching*, and it is the crux of how to attain the Taoist eternal truth. It is also the answer to how a Taoist could avoid danger and preserve life even during the aggressive, chaotic times of the warring states. Through the concepts of *te* and *wu-wei*, the Taoist found a way to live in the world and not contend with it, and at the same time accomplish whatever needs to be done.

Once the Taoist found a way to live safely within society, they moved to the final phase of their philosophy. This stage is best represented by the work of Chuang Tzu. He took all of the previous philosophy to the next level. Chuang Tzu is the first real philosopher that we can grab a hold of in the history of Taoism. We know that he lived from 369 BC to 286 BC, and he was a native of the state Meng during the last years of the warring states, where the violence of the time period was escalating to an all-time high. In response to this, he lived as a hermit, but became famous for his philosophical writings. The book titled *Chuang-tzu*, after this philosopher, was edited and put together formally by Kuo Hsiang; a famous commentator of the third century C.E.[12] This book's writing style is very different from the *Tao Te Ching*. Where the *Tao Te Ching* reads like a set of proverbs, Chuang Tzu's work consists of many allegorical stories with philosophical ideas dotted throughout.

Chuang Tzu's philosophy expounds on the idea of going beyond living in the realm of the worldly concerns. It is the ultimate goal of the Taoist and is typically deemed immortality. This concept was certainly touched on in the *Tao Te Ching*, but Chuang Tzu builds on and clarifies what the *Tao Te Ching* had to say. The concept of immortality is far from simple. Chuang Tzu explained it in various ways calling it entering the womb of the vital force, ascending to the cloudy heaven, dwelling in the place of mystery, or union with the Tao. The end goal is never really described in any detail, and has probably been seen differently by various Taoist groups. Some Taoists have seen immortality as a person leaving this world for the immortal realm with their body still in tact.

Others see it more as a mystical mystery of spirit or energies leaving the body to become one with the universe. However a Taoist views the end goal, they still all agree on the process necessary to attain it.

A person who has accomplished this goal is called a sage, or a perfect person. The first step in becoming a sage is to understand one's own nature given to them by the Tao. Remember, this is described as "*te*" in the *Tao Te Ching*. The Tao though doesn't give everything or everyone the same gifts. For example, birds and butterflies are granted the gift of flight, while horses are allocated the capacity for speed. When all are using their inherent abilities (*te*) to their fullest extent, things are naturally in rhythm with the Tao. According to Chang Tzu, in order to regain our innate abilities we must leave worldly attitudes behind. This does not infer that one has to opt out of society, but rather being able to look beyond the normal cultural conventions. One way to accomplish this is to ignore both praise and criticism. Instead, one is instructed to look within themselves to develop their own *te* that will help them figure out the way of the Tao. Chuang Tzu describes this as trusting the power of the Tao within.

> If you too go forward trusting to the Power (te) in you, taking the direction which accords with the Way, you will already have attained the utmost: why be so busy proclaiming Goodwill and Duty, like the man banging

the drum as he goes looking for runaways? Hmm, you are disrupting man's nature sir. (*Chuang-tzu* Chapter 13),[13]

Chang Tzu does not stop here, though. Even if we have attained our natural abilities, it does not mean we have become a sage yet. It is certainly an important first step, but becoming a sage is a very difficult process. To accomplish the goal, a person must move totally beyond themselves and become selfless; this is the supreme extension of the *wu-wei* concept of humility and weakness. At this point then, a sage has an ultimate view of reality unbiased by his own emotions. In this way, he transcends the petty and small, and is in line with the Tao. From this vantage point, he is able to see that in reality everything is actually one, since all things emanated from the same Tao.

> The 'world' is that in which the myriad of things are one. If you grasp the whole where they are one and assimilate yourself to it, the four limbs and hundred members will become dust and grime, and death and life, end and start, will became a daytime and a night, and nothing will be able to disturb you . . . (*Chuang-tzu* Chapter 21),[14]

It is this process of eradicating all selfish desires, and understanding the interconnectedness of all reality, that bonds one so strongly with the Tao; even upon death, they will be forever connected. That is immortality!

Chang Tao-ling, the founder of the Celestial Masters sect, imported all the Taoist philosophical ideas, but repackaged them into a more religious flavor, making them more understandable to the common person. One way this was accomplished was by employing the authority of Lord Lao (shortened name for Lao Tzu). Lao Tzu, the legendary author of the *Tao Te Ching*, had already been upgraded from a philosopher to a celestial power. This occurred in 150 AD when the Han Emperor dedicated a shrine to him and organized ceremonies in remembrance of him.[15] Chang Tao-ling took this a step further and believed Lord Lao was the deified Tao. The supreme Lord Lao then became the voice of the Tao, who spoke directly to Chang Tao-ling, giving him direction for his budding new church.

The *Tao Te Ching* was then transformed from a philosophical treatise into a holy scripture. Its wording style and complex ideas, however, made it difficult to understand. The Celestial Masters, therefore, created their own commentary that clarified this scripture for the average person. That document, called the *Xiang'er Commentary*, focused on two important issues that define the two parts of the Taoists' eternal truth. They are internal and external cultivation of the Tao. The outward behavior that was expected of people in the Celestial Masters group was laid out in twenty-seven precepts that were developed in the *Xiang'er Commentary*.[16] These laws revolved around the philosophical Taoist's concept of *wu-wei*, such as admonishing people to not act recklessly, to not seek fame, to not be obstinate, to not consider oneself inerrant, and to not contend with others. The sages of the *Tao Te Ching* time period seemed to effortlessly know how to apply *wu-wei* in all situations. The Celestial Masters, with their precepts, gave the common people information on how to accomplish the same task.

The Taoists don't split the internal and external part of our lives into two; they see them as intimately linked together. They feel one cannot properly cultivate the internal Tao without behaving in line with the principals of *wu-wei*. And it becomes easier to act according to *wu-wei* the more one nourishes the Tao within. The inner development of the Tao embraces the very essence of the Taoist fundament truth that the Tao is energy—the life source of everything. Taoists believe that prenatally, everyone has the energy, or *qi*, from the Tao flowing through their body, and regulating it perfectly. Beginning at birth, however, that energy begins to separate into three; these are deemed essence, vitality, and spirit. Each of these energies performs their own function, but they must work together as one. Essence is inherited from our parents; it is the fundamental energy of the body and is linked to one's actual flesh and blood. Vitality is an important force within our bodies that drives the processes that take place internally. Finally, our spirit is linked to our thoughts and our mind.[17] When essence, vitality, and Spirit energies become melded together, then a person is completely bonded with the Tao and all the cosmic forces. It is the completion of the journey toward immortality.

The Xiang'er Commentary tells the Taoist, "Those who concentrate their essences (energies) and do not act willfully (wu-wei) will never be forsaken by the powers of the Tao, they will become newborn."[18] The symbolism of the newborn imagery is very important in Taoism. It relates to both internal and external cultivation of the Tao. Internal nourishing of the Tao is, as discussed above, merging our energies to work together as they functioned as a newborn. Also, as we age, energies are drained due to pressures and worries that accumulate over time. Babies, on the other hand, represent a pure state with all energy intact. Being as a newborn is as distant form death as one can get; therefore, a baby represents life at its fullest. Recall that the external behavior is based on the concept wu-wei, or non-action. Newborns naturally have no contention with the world yet. They are not self-conscious and so have not developed the concept of "I" or "that is mine." Except for the basic needs for food and love, newborns have no desires yet. Also, all their movements are free and spontaneous with no ill will towards others; they are a prime example of wu-wei.

As we age though, we accumulate desires and contend with the world, all the while draining our energies and separating them more and more each day. The Taoist sees the separation of the energies as a division between mind and body with the yin and yang no longer working as they should in harmony together. Our mind is our spiritual energy, and our body contains essence and vitality. When these do not function together, a person moves further away from the Tao. For example, when a person does not think before they act and indulges their bodily impulses, then this could lead to such behaviors as illicit sex or overeating. The mind and body must be in sync with each other for the Tao spirit to flow internally, reshaping and reforming a person from the inside out. The Celestial Masters' *Xiang'er Commentary* tells the Taoist, "When the (internal) spirits are formed, pneumas come to carry and manage the human body. If you wish to complete this task, do not depart form the One. The One is the Tao."[19] The pneumas here represent the primal energy of the Tao living fully within the body, and governing it perfectly as if it was a newborn. A later scripture, *Awakening of the Tao*, describes the same thing:

> If you want to know the true seed of essence and life, it is nothing but the original, innate, primal, true unified energy. This energy is imperceptible and ungraspable Internalized it is true emptiness; externalized it is ineffable existence. It cannot be communicated in words, cannot be depicted in writing. If we were to insist on an

illustration, it would simply be a circle. When names are force on it, Confucians call it the absolute, Buddhists call it complete awareness, Taoists call it the gold pill… This alone is the true seed of essence and life.[20]

The gold pill is symbolic for a new consciousness that is completely in line with the Tao. It only develops once a person's mind and body are in harmony. Obtaining the golden pill is the completion of internal cultivation; after which is just the easy task of maintaining the Tao within.

When pursuing through the history of Taoism, it is easy to see that it has attracted a wide variety of an outlandish number of gods and occult-like ideas that has given the impression that underneath all the fluff, their lies nothing of value. Because Taoism deals specifically with supernatural forces, it has naturally drawn some people who have extreme ideas about the transcendental. Adding to the problem, the Taoist never developed a head figure who could make decisions on what is orthodox. Over the years, the problem has escalated. With each new sect, new scripture was simply added to the older ones. That is why the Taoist canon has over 1000 various scriptures in it, making it one of the largest volumes of sacred scripture. A random look through the various scriptures of the Taoism would give anyone one a very fuzzy picture of what this religion believes is important. Each sect has their own practices and rituals; and even if they share the same rituals, they may have different meanings.

The main sects today, however, keep their focus on internal cultivation. It is always understood, though, that the internal cultivation leads to better behavior based on the principals of *wu-wei*. The inner nourishing of the Tao is a Taoist's fullest expression of their eternal truth of the Tao as a source of energy that brings forth all of life. It is by focusing on their own internal energies that a Taoist finds a direct connection to the Tao, leading to living in the flow with the cosmic forces, or in other words, acting in accordance with *wu-wei*. Taoists focus on living in the present and in balance with the forces of nature that are created by the Tao. They have faith that their constant nourishing of life's forces will give them a long, healthy life now, and in the future they will be rewarded with an eternal connection to the Tao. "If you want to practice this Way, you must do it in the creative evolution of yin and yang and of heaven and earth, realize its experience in the midst of all things and all events, and practice and hold it in the presences of all people. This is work that is alive, effervescent, free-liberated, gloriously enlightened, true, and great." (*Awakening of the Tao*)[21] It is how a Taoist avoids empty goals and the normal rushing about for frivolous things. They focus on the important thing and that is nourishing life; that is the Tao itself.

BIBLIOGRAPHY

1. Hendrischke, Barbara. *The Taiping Jing and the Beginnings of Daoism*. Los Angeles: University of California Press, 2006. p. 116-117

2. Ibid., p. 32

3. Wildish, Paul. *Principals of Taoism*. London: Thorsons, 2000. p. 44

4. Brokenkamp, Stephen, R. *Early Daoist Scriptures*. Berkeley: University of California Press, 1997. p. 165

5. Graham, A. C. *Chuang-Tzu, The Inner Chapters*. Indianapolis: Hackett Publishing Company, Inc., 1989. p. 4

6. Yu-Lan, Fung. *A Short History of Chinese Philosophy*. New York: The Free Press, 1976. p. 30

7. Ibid., p. 61

8. Ibid., p. 61-62

9. Robinet, Isabelle. *Taoism, Growth of a Religion*. Stanford: Stanford University Press, 1997. p. 26

10. Kirkland, Russell. *Taoism, the Enduring Tradition*. New York: Routledge Taylor & Francis Group, 2004. p. 61

11. Thorpy, Michael J., M.D., and Jan Yager, Ph.D. *The Encyclopedia of Sleep and Sleep Disorders*. New York: Facts on File, Inc., 2001. p 196-197

12. Yu-Lan, p. 104

13. Graham, p. 128

14. Graham, p. 131

15. Wildish, p. 43

BIBLIOGRAPHY

16. Bokenkamp, p. 49-51

17. Wildish, p.17-18

18. Brokenkamp, p. 124-125

19. Brokenkamp, p. 89

20. Clearly, Thomas. *The Taoist Classics, Volume 3*. Boston: Shambhala, 2003. p. 507

21. Ibid., p. 524

CHAPTER 8:
CONCLUSION

Through the pages of this book we have traveled a great journey together from China to the forests of India, and from the deserts of Saudi Arabia to the temple of Jerusalem. The closer look at each faith has clarified their own rich background with important events, places, literature, and prominent figures that helped give vitality and breadth to their understanding of God. This book has purposely tried to celebrate the various ways that each religion understands God in order to show that diversity doesn't have to be scary, and it doesn't have to separate people. Accepting each others differences is one of the best ways to show respect for others. The world needs not more of one religion, but an acceptance of all true faiths. This book has only covered the six major religions, but in no way does it exclude the others that may have fewer followers. But are all religions valid simply because they exist? I don't think so. The question is how do we know which spiritual paths are for real and which ones are false? The answer lies in what the religion teaches and how the practitioners behave due to those teachings.

Religion, in other words, has implications on human behavior. If God is truly found in a religion, then it should lead its adherents to good, ethical behavior. In today's modern times, too many secularists have concluded that morality is like a shape shifter that can change depending on the time period or culture. Certainly, people's ideas and lifestyles are different from Africa to America, and the type of life lived today is different from the historical past. The truth about ethics, though, does not have to become entangled in theoretical jargon. It is simple; morality is having compassion for yourself and others. That reality does not change no matter where or when you live.

Is there ever an excuse for adultery, cheating, stealing, or murder? I don't think so. The origin of these problems stems from hate, frustration, a drive for success, or lack of control over one's life. These powerful feelings consume too much of our daily lives and lead us to selfishness and misery, instead of toward God. Religion's job is to extract these toxins from our lives. Knowing God can also act as a buffer for when life gets difficult, so that a person can endure hard times and still behave in a compassionate way. How does this happen? It occurs because true devotees of each of the different religions develop a unique relationship with God.

Jews enjoy a covenantal connection with God. Recall that this covenant is based on the Law, which lays out the moral expectations for the adherents of Judaism. Faith is another important aspect of the covenant. For Jews, this is an awesome trust in God that he is always acting for the best interest of humanity. Even in the worst of times, Jews still cling to their covenant and hope that things will improve for them. This idea is summed up in the Messianic age—a time in the future when the Messiah will emerge and peace will settle over the earth. Jews, as a nation, have endured incredible persecution. They were dominated by other nations for many years and fought several wars to try to win their freedom. Furthermore, they have been the victim of racism and even tortured in the holocaust. It is their complete trust in God that has helped them survive to this day.

Muhammad taught the Muslims that "There is no God but God." This simple statement is the creed by which Muslims live their lives. A belief in only one God stimulates feelings of gratitude towards God for creating them and the entire world. A Muslim believes that since God is our Creator, we can only become the fulfilled people we were destined to be by living in unison with God's plans. Too many times people get lost in their own gods or their own goals that they set up for themselves such as fame, power, and financial success. Muslims put God first in their life. They are constantly striving against their evil inclinations in order to do God's will. The Sharia'ah Law, especially the five pillars of wisdom, helps them stay focused on what they call the straight path. Muslims come to know God and his ways intimately by studying his different attributes, which are explained in the Qu'ran. They dedicate their lives to God with faith that in the end, they will be rewarded for their efforts.

Recall that Jesus preached about spreading the "kingdom of God," meaning to bring God's peace and love to the world. Because God loves us, Jesus proclaimed, we should love others as well. To this day, Christians continue doing the work of creating the "kingdom of God" on earth. Even when challenges come their way, they stay on the right course because they are empowered with God's grace. Christians who feel filled up with God's love, and have a deep connection to God, live a grace-filled life. This entails the Holy Spirit living in their hearts, warming them to God's love from the inside. Some Christians may also call this having Jesus in their heart, as really Jesus and the Holy Spirit are part of the same trinity. Either way, the outcome is the same; they gain the ability to endure any hardships. This can be seen in the martyrs of the early church who where willing to face death rather then turn away from Christianity.

Hindu's believe they are intimately connected to God through their soul. Coming to realize this is called God-consciousness or self-realization, and obtaining it leads to ultimate bliss and salvation. Though many may understand this intellectually, it takes a lot of spiritual work to come to feel and act on that knowledge that our souls are linked with God. For Hindus, there are four paths or yogas that can guide a person to God-consciousness; these include knowledge (jnana), meditation (raja), devotion (bhakti), and action (karma). These paths are made for different types of people, but they all have the same purpose. That is, they guide a person into alignment with God's plans, and so that person naturally creates harmony and peace in the world. In other words, yoga helps one act according to their true dharma which results in salvation.

Buddhists' connection to ultimate reality is called enlightenment. This state of mind can not be obtained by an immoral person. To reach enlightenment, one has to eliminate greed, anger, and ignorance. According to the Buddha, the first step toward this goal is proper moral behavior, which then sets up a person to accrue positive karma instead of the negative type. Once this much is done, a person can work on concentration, mindfulness, and the development of wisdom which ultimately leads to nirvana—everlasting peace.

The Taoists call their relationship with the divine "being in the flow with the Tao," and it can be achieved by practicing both internal and external cultivation of the Tao. They personally experience God within their bodies as the energy flowing within them. When this energy is working as it should, through proper mixing of the yin and the yang, then they are in harmony with the Tao, and therefore, the world. This leads a Taoist to naturally abide by *wu-wie*; that is, they are selfless, non-contending, and living a simple life in sync with the Tao.

For each of the different religions, the path to a relationship with God starts out the same—by perfecting ones moral values. Our world is full of beautifully good people who come from all of the various religions. The lingo for their moral training might have different names such as spreading the kingdom of God, dharma, *wu-wie*, the straight path, the Law, or ethics training, but they all teach the same philosophy that one must be gentle, selfless, content, and lead a simple life. Once a person has set aside their vices and evil inclinations, then, and only then, can a person build a strong bond with the Divine. This rapport with God might be called by different names such as a grace-filled life, enlightenment, in flow with the Tao, God-consciousness, or submission to a single God, yet it results in the same thing—a person who is living a new life where they automatically gain strength and endurance for tough times. They experience less anger, frustration and lose the drive for financial gain, but rather focus on spiritual success. This is why they are happy, gentler people who live an ethical life. One cannot be connected to God and do otherwise. Any one of the paths described by the six major religions will lead a person to this destination.

The deepest, strongest bond with the Divine, though, is made by encompassing all the different religious paths, so that the Divine penetrates into every aspect of one's life. If we combine all the various definitions of who God is, the result is a single God who created everything and continues to pervade, uphold, and maintain that Creation. Furthermore, he is a God of love, peace, and dwells in the hearts and minds of all his Creation. Wow, what a vision of God that is! Understanding each of the faiths helps us to see the grander picture of God.